TO UNITE OUR STRENGTH

Enhancing the United Nations Peace and Security System

By
John M. Lee
Robert von Pagenhardt
and
Timothy W. Stanley

Foreword by
Robert S. McNamara

UNIVERSITY
PRESS OF
AMERICA

Lanham • New York • London

INTERNATIONAL
ECONOMIC
STUDIES
INSTITUTE
Washington, D.C.

Copyright © 1992 by
University Press of America®, Inc.
4720 Boston Way
Lanham, Maryland 20706

3 Henrietta Street
London WC2E 8LU England

Co-published by arrangement with the
International Economic Studies Institute

Library of Congress Cataloging-in-Publication Data

Lee, John M.
To unite our strength : enhancing the United Nations peace and
security system / John M. Lee, Robert Von Pagenhardt,
Timothy W. Stanley.
p.   cm.
Includes bibliographical references.
1. United Nations—Armed Forces.   2. International police.
I. Pagenhardt, Robert von.   II. Stanley, Timothy W.
III. International Economic Studies Institute (Washington, D.C.)
IV. Title.
JX1981.P7L42   1992   341.5'8—dc20   92–26899 CIP

ISBN 0–8191–8865–4 (cloth : alk. paper)
ISBN 0–8191–8866–2 (pbk. : alk. paper)

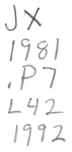
". . . strengthening the UN's capacity for peacemaking, peacekeeping, and
peace enforcement should be a top priority for the United States
in the post-Cold War world. Nothing could more directly
serve America's interests, or that of the larger
international community, than fulfilling the
goal of collective security laid out
in the UN Charter forty-seven
years ago."*

Cyrus R. Vance
Personal Envoy of the United Nations Secretary-General
Former United States Secretary of State and Deputy Secretary of Defense

* Statement before the Senate Committee on Governmental Affairs,
Washington, D.C., June 9, 1992.

TABLE OF CONTENTS

FOREWORD

The post-Cold War era is unexpectedly complex and challenging. Not only have there been new acts of aggression, as in the case of Iraq, but the seeds of old ethnic and religious quarrels have sprouted as the Soviet empire collapsed. Across the globe, factions, separatists and ethnic groups pursue agendas that carry implicit threats to the peace. The economic and development gaps between North and South continue to widen, aggravated by exploding populations and civil strife and the uneven spread of technology. Social as well as economic justice is absent in much of the world, and new uncertainties loom about serious environmental damage to the planet itself.

Not all the news is bad: the spread of democracy and the movement toward a better balance between the market and state regulation are proving contagious. Moreover, as both developed and developing countries phase down military programs, human, scientific, and financial resources will become available for application elsewhere. But without a vision of the post-Cold War world -- a framework of international order and security -- it will be difficult to utilize the new resources to maximum advantage.

Many international organizations have roles in the post-Cold War world, including some military entities like NATO, but most have geographic or functional limitations. Only the United Nations family has a universal mandate. No other organization or country, even the United States, can enforce peace across the globe. That is why this analysis is so timely and important. In it, the authors conclude that, although the United Nations needs restructuring, it can develop into a system encompassing preventive diplomacy, crisis management, peacekeeping and peace-enforcement -- thereby helping to fill the gap between the real and ideal world.

The authors, Messrs. Lee, von Pagenhardt and Stanley have had extensive international security experience. Their proposals, which draw on that experience, deserve serious consideration both at the United Nations and in world capitals.

Robert S. McNamara

PREFACE

The preamble to the Charter of the United Nations begins:

> "We the Peoples of the United Nations
> Determined to save succeeding generations from
> the scourge of war . . . . *to unite our strength* to
> maintain international *peace and security* . . . ."

We have taken the title of this book from the words italicized in the preamble and dedicate it to the revitalizing of the UN system that will make them attainable.

This is very much a team effort, drawing on extensive and varied experience at the United Nations itself and in NATO and several U.S. agencies concerned with international security. The three principal authors, whose biographies appear at the end of the book, combine over a century of public service. We have been aided throughout by the insights of Ambassador James Leonard, former Deputy U.S. Representative at the UN and Irving Pfefferblit, a retired UN civil servant. Major contributions were also made by the Institute's editor, retired U.S. foreign affairs specialist Albert P. Toner, and research associate Lukas Haynes, whose analytic and production skills have been invaluable.

Although all of the above happen to be Americans, we have consistently sought an international perspective and solicited comments from a variety of experts from other countries. For example, we arranged three review conferences: one involved international senior military officers attending the Naval Postgraduate School's Defense Resources Management Institute at Monterey, California in February, 1992; another took place at UN headquarters in New York in April as a Non-Government Organizations

Disarmament Forum with an international panel and audience;[1] and the third, also in April, assembled a small group of U.S. experts from the Washington policy community. Each of the principal authors has also consulted widely and spoken on the topic to groups in his own area.[2]

The International Economic Studies Institute (IESI) is a nonprofit and strictly nonpartisan research organization in Washington, D.C., which has been classified by the IRS as a publicly supported (501c3) entity to which all contributions are tax-deductible. IESI takes its motto from Woodrow Wilson's dictum that "we are participants, whether we would or not, in the life of the world."

This study might seem somewhat afield from IESI's normal focus upon the intersections of international economic, political, and security issues. We undertook it because of a particular conviction that the only path to sustainable economic progress on a global basis is for countries to redirect resources away from wasteful military competition toward economic goals. For that to happen, the security concerns of the post-Cold War world must be addressed; and a revitalized United Nations -- with military enforcement as well as peacekeeping and peacemaking capabilities -- is the only body able to tackle them globally under the rule of international law. The Trustees of the Institute, listed inside the back cover, encouraged the study in this belief, although they should not be held accountable for the book's conclusions.

The research for this project at IESI was supported in part by a grant from the United States Institute of Peace. The opinions, findings, and conclusions or recommendations in this book are those of the authors and do not necessarily reflect the views of the United States Institute of Peace -- or any other part of the U.S. Government, although the authors hope that Government may come to accept some of them. This financial support and contributions from the Joyce Mertz-Gilmore Foundation of New York and others are acknowledged with appreciation.

While we cannot list the many civilian and military officials, past and present, who shared their wisdom we must acknowledge our debt to them collectively -- and anonymously, as some preferred. Peer review is a normal Institute practice and we owe special thanks to our independent reviewers who read the advance summary[3] published in April, namely Edison W. Dick Esq., President of the United Nations Association, National Capital Area Division, Ambassador Geoffrey A.H. Pearson, former Canadian Ambassador for Disarmament, and General Indar Jit Rikhye, Indian Army (Ret.), who is currently a Fellow at the U.S. Institute of Peace. They must, of course, be exonerated from any responsibility for our conclusions.

We are particularly grateful to Robert S. McNamara, former U.S. Secretary of Defense and World Bank President for his foreword. Finally, we wish to thank our publishers, the University Press of America, and Ms. Maureen Muncaster in particular, for their cooperation in making a rapid transition from manuscript to book.

In the very nature of a cooperative effort among writers in California, Florida, New York, and Washington, and under deadlines imposed by an exceptionally timely subject, someone must assume responsibility for the final product and any deficiencies it contains. That obligation falls to the undersigned as project director and President of the Institute. However, the credit for what we hope will make a valuable contribution to international discourse belongs to all who have shared in the preparation of this book.

Timothy W. Stanley
President
International Economic Studies Institute

TO UNITE OUR STRENGTH

OVERVIEW

This study was undertaken with the conviction that the end of the Cold War, the successful UN operation for the restoration of Kuwait, and the current UN effort to establish legitimate government in Cambodia could presage a new era for international peacekeeping, for international institution building and the securing of peace. Clearly, if nations of the world so decide, they can employ the UN for the enforcement of security and peace.

The authors recognize that international order and world peace involve many aspects of human and governmental activity beyond the military, and that tasks must be performed by governments and the UN organization beyond security as traditionally defined. Indeed, some voices call for new definitions of "security" to include economic and even environmental issues. These other matters lie, however, beyond the focus of this analysis.

Continued outbreaks of violence around the world show no lessening of the need for common action to "maintain international peace and security," the first UN purpose proclaimed in the Charter, now that the discipline enforced by the East-West confrontation has evaporated. Existing international mechanisms for the purpose of assuring security, however, are not adequate. The past ad hoc systems developed for the Korean and Kuwait "police actions," with their massive and largely American deployment of military power overseas and their predominant U.S. direction are unlikely to be repeated. Another such operation would almost certainly be unacceptable, both to the U.S. public and government and to world authorities and peoples. A U.S. role as world policeman is not likely to be an admissible solution, here or abroad. Nor can other powers or regional groups play that part. Europe is preoccupied with its unification and eastern accommodation; the USSR has dissolved and its republics are beset with political, economic and military crises; Japan, while a world-class economic power, lacks the necessary support to play the lead role, even in its own area, if it were willing to do so.

There remains the United Nations. Nearly half a century after its Charter was signed, the organization and system created "to save succeeding generations from the scourge of war" falls far short of the founders' vision. The end of the Cold War and the unblocking of the Security Council, however, have made progress possible. The time seems ripe for a renewed effort to develop the UN into an effective central mechanism for maintaining international peace and security. Full development will be a monumental task, requiring major and time-consuming revisions in concepts, procedures, and structures. But the goal is essential, for the United Nations is the only global security framework available.

The UN Charter rightly places its first priority on "peaceful settlement of disputes."   Chapter VI provides a number of means for the pacific settlement of disputes: negotiation, enquiry, mediation, conciliation, arbitration, and judicial settlement -- with special reference to the International Court of Justice. It is noteworthy that the Security Council retains the right at any stage to recommend procedures or "terms of settlement" (Articles 36 and 37) when the dispute is likely to "endanger the maintenance of international peace and security."   The Council may presumably take further action under Chapter VII.

Legalities aside, however, no actions by the UN or other international body are likely to succeed over the long term unless rooted in the acceptance, however reluctant, of the parties themselves. We therefore regard the imminent threat or use of force by the UN as a last resort when other means have failed.

Nevertheless, the potential availability of military forces under the UN can, if credible, act as a powerful incentive to reach peaceful settlements and to deter acts which might otherwise result in actual UN deployments. Serbian behavior, in the spring and summer of 1992, is a case in point; as long as there was no credible threat of outside military intervention by the UN, NATO, the Conference on Security and Cooperation in Europe (CSCE) or the European Community, the Serbs remained free to pursue their objectives by military force alone, without regard for the opposition of the international community.

The probability remains that from time to time, the actual use of UN military forces as a deterrent threat and in combat will ultimately be required when other means have failed, or if a government or faction persists in defying Security Council resolutions in the face of overwhelming international condemnation. Iraq's aggression is a case in point and the former Yugoslavia illustrates the consequences of apparent UN toothlessness. Many lesser possibilities may arise: to support peacekeepers under attack; to enforce IAEA inspections of nuclear installations; to rescue masses of refugees; or to reinforce the forces defending the borders of a nation under hostile threat. (Later chapters will discuss the difficult case of internal civil wars and anarchy, which are increasingly the source of conflict in the post-Cold War world.)

This book concentrates on strengthening the military elements of a stronger United Nations for enhancing world peace and security, without prejudice to the many other components of the UN's overall activities. A voluminous literature is available on those components, whereas military enforcement has been less intensively studied.

The authors do not wish to convey the impression that proposals to implement the Charter's collective security provisions are a new concept. On the contrary, over the years, UN officials, various governments and many non-governmental organizations (NGOs) have circulated ideas on improving peacekeeping, implementing Article 43, and even creating a standing military force. As recently as the Carter Administration, the U.S. submitted proposals on establishing a peacekeeping reserve, improving airlift capacity, and helping to improve logistics, although it specifically rejected the concept of a standing UN force. However, rather than merely analyzing past proposals, we have tried to address the crucial areas needed to build a comprehensive *system*, without which the UN cannot handle even its present range and intensity of international engagement. In doing so, we must acknowledge the many serious prior efforts to improve the UN's capacity for peacemaking, peacekeeping, and peace-enforcement.[1]

On June 17, 1992 Secretary-General Boutros Boutros-Ghali issued his response to the mandate from the Security Council Heads of Government at their January 31 meeting, the first ever held at Summit level. This report, "An Agenda for Peace"[2] represents important progress over traditional United Nations thinking in two respects.

First, the Secretary-General seeks to integrate into a comprehensive system all of the many components of preventive diplomacy, peacekeeping and peacemaking, in contrast to some attempts in the past to compartmentalize them, bureaucratically or politically. Second, he deals specifically with peace-enforcement, first by calling for implementation of Article 43, recognizing that this will require time, and then by proposing as a provisional measure, specially constituted or heavily armed peace-enforcement units.

Although, as a conceptual paper rather than a structural plan, the report is short on operational and logistic details, it does break new ground. We hope that our book can help provide such detailed suggestions for the implementation phase. But a retrospective look may be helpful.

The military structure built into the UN Charter was designed with World War II fresh in mind. The vision was of a United Nations opposed by a powerful aggressor, a Hitler, for example, starting World War III. The Security Council's function was to determine high strategy, as dealt with at wartime summit conferences like Casablanca and Yalta. The Military Staff Committee would resemble the Combined Chiefs of Staff, collectively converting summit decisions into broad strategic directives to an Eisenhower-like theater commander and then returning individually to their capitals to implement the necessary national support. The theater commander, in the field, had the hour by hour task of converting the Chiefs' directives into operational orders and conducting the operations.

Our study finds that the basic UN military concept provides a workable foundation, so that the Charter needs no revision of its military provisions. What is needed, however, is the development of organizations, relationships, and practices to allow the UN to conduct military operations effectively. The operations required may be of virtually any nature and size. The structure must accommodate international peacekeeping, ranging from virtually non-combat, largely constabulary operations under Chapter VI of the Charter to international enforcement action under Chapter VII, involving the threat or the reality of combat at any of a wide span of types, magnitudes and levels of intensity. To meet the vision of the founders, it is essential that the direction and command of UN forces be truly and visibly international, not merely an operation by the U.S. or others with some UN gloss.

To meet these problems, the UN needs improvement, first, in military direction and command, and, second, in provision of forces, facilities, and support. In the first area, the principal need is for a single, central Executive Agency, adequately staffed, charged with carrying out the operational directions of the Security Council and any relevant guidance from the Military Staff Committee that the Security Council transmits. Neither the Security Council nor the Military Staff Committee can effectively perform the executive function. They are committees whose products are resolutions arrived at by time-consuming discussion and compromise. They cannot control a complex, moving situation requiring day and night, moment by moment decisions and actions. Their function must be to give broad guidance to and oversee the performance of the executive. Nor can a military commander in the field, whether at a theater or a lower level, handle the overall UN Executive Agent's role. A civilian official, able to control and coordinate political as well as military elements, and implement the Security Council's purposes is essential.

As discussed further in Chapter Two, the Executive Agent should be the Secretary-General, who has in practice acted in that capacity for the UN's peacekeeping (Chapter VI) operations. Even for peacekeeping and non-combat peacemaking, however, his present operational staff is inadequately manned or trained and therefore ineffective for military enforcement operations -- where the Executive Agent must be able to prepare, launch, operate, and support combat forces. The Secretary-General must therefore be given an ample and expert UN Military Staff for the whole range of his military functions, if he is to discharge his proper role.

That body, separate from the existing Military Staff Committee, should be led by a Chief of Staff, a senior officer of international reputation, appointed by the Secretary-General (SG) and reporting directly to him and his principal deputy for peacekeeping and security. The Military Staff itself, also appointed by the SG, should be adequate in numbers and qualifications and properly trained and equipped both to man UN Headquarters and to provide supporting elements for field commanders' staffs.

The Chief of Staff and all members of the Military Staff must be unequivocally international in their functioning. Like other members of the Secretariat, they should "not seek nor receive instructions from any government or from any other authority external to the Organization" and should "refrain from any action which might reflect on their position as international officials responsible only to the Organization." [3]

The United Nations' ultimate goal should be to build the capacity for Executive Agency into the Secretariat for operations on any scale. Until that is achieved, however, operations might be required of a magnitude, complexity, or simultaneity beyond the Secretary-General's then-existing capacity to direct. In such cases, as a provisional measure of last resort only, the Security Council might have to designate as its Executive Agent the head of a member government having available the necessary national and military resources. To insure that the UN's control and direction of such operations is effective and recognized, the Security Council must establish the relationships needed between the UN and any national Executive Agent, and should formalize agreements thereon with potential Agents -- to include nations other than the U.S. All participants should insure the unmistakably international nature of such an operation.

In addition to the Executive Agent, whether he be at UN Headquarters or a national capital, each operation must have a UN commander on the scene. For large multi-service operations, the field commander may need considerable experience and wide acceptance by subordinates and peers. Presumably a four star General, the Commander will require a substantial staff and resources like those deployed by General MacArthur in Korea and General Schwarzkopf in the Persian Gulf. Lesser tasks, of course, have lesser needs. The workable solution is to tailor each field command to fit its specific operation, drawing the needed elements from the forces which nations would earmark for UN assignment under Article 43. The U.S., for example, might earmark elements of its Central Command, and other nations such command resources as they could make available. As noted above, the UN Military Staff should also provide some personnel resources to the field commander, to insure effective liaison. This approach appears consonant with Article 47(3) of the Charter.

The second area where the UN military system needs development is in the provision of forces and support for UN operations. At present, the Charter provisions for enforcement operations do not function, and the system for peacekeeping could be improved. This study makes recommendations for earmarking, preparing, and operating national forces for UN service under Charter Articles 43 and 45, and for facilities, support, and assistance that could be called for under the general assistance Articles 48 and 49. All these Articles are in Chapter VII, referring to "action with respect to threats to the peace, breaches of the peace, and acts of aggression."

The system proposed by the authors would also improve the

availability, training, flexibility, direction, control, and support of the peacekeeping elements performing non-combat UN operations. With the improvement in the UN Secretariat and supporting communications and infrastructure, the peacekeepers could respond more efficiently to changes in the nature and requirements of the situation. They could do so without compromise to the non-combat nature or political control of those peacekeeping and peacemaking operations.

A new element would be a standing UN force, herein called the UN Legion. Initially, it is conceived as a relatively small, combat capable ground element of brigade-plus size (about 5,000 men) perhaps supported by limited tactical air and modest naval units, but the force would be expanded to three reinforced light brigades if the experiment proves successful. The key element of such a Legion would be its composition, not of national military units but of individual volunteers seconded to the UN from the armed forces of most, if not all, of the UN countries. Thus, while serving the UN, these military personnel would have a collective loyalty only to the UN. The Legion would operate directly under the authority of the Security Council, with command exercised by the Legion Commander through the Secretary-General and the Chief of Staff. Therefore, the Legion would be immediately available for commitment alone in smaller contingencies or in advance of or reinforcement of other formations.

The strictly international character of a UN Legion and its quick response capacity should make it more readily usable than national elements. It could be of great value in showing the UN flag, establishing a tripwire boundary, making a key reinforcement, or firing a figurative shot across the bow. Furthermore, establishing a standing Legion would educate the UN in the problems of purely international military forces, and thus be a test of the vision of a UN ultimately able to carry larger responsibilities for maintaining peace and security.

There are two essential differences between this proposal and the peace-enforcement units recommended by Boutros-Ghali on June 17, 1992. Whereas the Legion would have a unique international identity and be available on a permanent basis, his report calls for national units on-call to be summoned by the Security Council. The authors are confident that the advantages of better coordination, enhanced credibility, and quicker response would soon emerge from a preliminary one-brigade experiment with a UN

Legion. National forces might, however, be useful provisional measures, as his report suggests.

Because the concept of a standing UN combat-capable force has not been seriously examined by the United Nations since Secretary-General Trygvie Lie first requested a "United Nations guard" in 1948-49, this study devotes substantial analysis to the nature, practicality, and value of such a UN Legion.

The largest proportion of UN operational forces will necessarily have to come from national elements earmarked by the nations for UN duty under Charter Articles 43 and 45. Earmarking of certain forces by major states was undertaken as soon as the UN was organized, but the process was wrecked on the shoals of the Cold War. Originally, the concept was to use mostly forces from the permanent members of the Security Council. But, in the methods that have been improvised over the years for manning peacekeeping operations, large nations' forces have been virtually excluded to avoid the intrusion of Cold War or hegemonic concerns. It is now possible and desirable to reach agreements under Articles 43 and 45 with all the UN nations and regional international organizations that have potentially useful resources. In the aggregate, the UN would then have a current, worldwide encyclopedia of the forces, facilities, bases, and military assistance that nations had agreed to provide on the Security Council's call, with an evaluation of their capabilities, condition, and readiness.

Presumably, nations will insist on concurring in the passage of forces to UN control at the time they are actually called, in accordance with each nation's constitutional requirements. However, to speed response to rapidly breaking situations, we call for Quick Reaction Forces (QRF) sufficient to constitute in aggregate one air transportable corps of ground forces with air and naval support and one follow-on sea transportable mechanized corps.

Members of an enlarged Security Council structure would be asked to pledge, in advance, a portion of their earmarked units for the Quick Reaction Force, to be provided on immediate call, subject only to "overriding" national emergency. In principle, we think it reasonable for each permanent member to provide one QRF division each with ancillary units and each other member of the proposed Peace Management Committee to contribute one brigade or equivalent to the QRF. Such contributions should in our view be made at no cost to the UN's strained budget. They would be, in effect, the price of admission to the expanded Security Council structure described in later chapters. The actual composition would have to be reviewed by the UN Military Staff in the light of foreseeable challenges or threats.

In addition to the elements which members earmark for the UN, nations will have military forces, facilities, and support capabilities which may be needed on occasion, and which should be "declared" to the UN Military Staff for contingency planning. The Charter's general assistance provisions (Articles 48 and 49) enable the Security Council to call for any such resources for specific operations and for such general, on-going requirements as support for semi-permanent peacekeeping operations and for bases and transport for the Legion. Matters of this nature that can be anticipated should be negotiated in advance.

These measures would facilitate effective contingency preplanning, force design and selection, and operational planning, control, and support for UN operations at all levels of size and intensity for peacemaking, peacekeeping, or enforcement. They would also form the basis for developing UN standards for training, readiness, and communications necessary to permit forces from many nations to operate together.

This study explores the practicalities of creating a UN peace and security system combining political and command direction and flexible force structures along the foregoing lines. The term "system" is used advisedly. We had planned to look at alternative options for UN military forces, ranging from executive agency to standing elements and then to on-call forces. However, analysis of the problem, supplemented by discussions with numerous experts, convinced us that no one option would be sufficient. Rather a system is required, combining the flexibility noted above with reforms to the Security Council and the Secretariat to facilitate preventive diplomacy and crisis management as well as military measures of varied intensity.

This book starts with an overview of the United Nations in the new era it has entered, its limitations and opportunities, and the need for a more representative Security Council structure. Chapters Two and Three describe, respectively, the military and the UN Headquarters changes needed for the new comprehensive system.

Chapter Four examines relevant lessons from the past, such as NATO's experience with international forces and staffs and the work done exploring the proposal for a NATO Multilateral Force, and the UN's own learning curve in peacemaking and peacekeeping. In addition, the chapter draws on past lessons to consider the practical problems the UN might face in the creation of a UN Legion and suggests solutions.

Chapter Five examines how the proposed system might work in a difficult situation, such as the break-up of Yugoslavia, given a variety of UN options and the necessary planning and preparation. Chapter Six explores the critical area of financing UN peacekeeping and enforcement. Chapter Seven summarizes the conclusions and recommendations.

The authors recognize that a sizable body of opinion within the UN community opposes in principle the creation of UN military capabilities beyond consensual peacekeeping, believing that the UN should be restricted to peaceful means. We, however, believe with the UN's founders that the existence of a system such as we propose will make peaceful settlements more attainable, and that when force must be used in the interest of peace, it is better that we unite our strength under the UN flag than through national governments, even if the latter have some UN approval.

If experience can overcome the lack of confidence many governments now profess in the United Nations, then in the new century there may evolve a UN system capable of maintaining peace or restoring security largely on its own. That would enable governments, in turn, to reallocate some of the resources now devoted to military security to other human and environmental needs. But, as Robert McNamara notes in his foreword, the availability and use of such resources requires a "vision" and a "framework of international order and security." We hope that this book will contribute to those needs.

CHAPTER ONE

THE UNITED NATIONS IN A NEW ERA

The UN's Role: A Perspective

Despite its poor record on major world security issues during the years of Cold War paralysis,* the United Nations proved surprisingly resilient as it became evident that the era of confrontation was drawing to a close. Under the leadership of outgoing Secretary-General Javier Perez de Cuellar, who surprised critics of his allegedly "colorless" style, the UN achieved some real accomplishments in diplomacy and peacekeeping ranging from the follow-up missions in Iraq to ending the hostage crisis in Lebanon, and obtaining breakthroughs in the obstacles to peace in the Western Sahara, Namibia, El Salvador, and Cambodia.

The five permanent members of the Security Council have also managed to maintain a common stance among themselves and with the full Council on most key issues since Mikhail Gorbachev announced (appropriately, in his 1986 address to the UN itself) the Soviet Union's "New Thinking." In particular, the Soviet Union supported the Gulf coalition, at least after its own last-minute peacemaking efforts with its former Iraqi client

---

* The Korean War must be treated as an exception, since the UN's role was allowed by the USSR's fortuitous absence from the Security Council which permitted it to authorize assistance for the Republic of Korea; and after the USSR's return, the General Assembly's taking charge, exemplified by passage of the Uniting for Peace resolution. In fact, if not in theory, this was a United States operation in which the senior U.S. field commanders also wore a UN hat, although it was supported by contingents of allied forces, e.g., from Europe, South Asia, Turkey and Australia.

failed. Communist China acquiesced in the majority consensus and sent a small contingent of officers to participate in the post cease-fire Kurdish relief effort -- the first time in UN history that all five permanent members had taken part in a field operation.

All of this obviously augurs well for the potential growth of the UN system. But as noted in the Overview, much will have to be done to ensure its accomplishment. This study approaches such a revised system by building on the provisions for international security laid down in the UN Charter. It proposes to build new structures administratively in order to cope more effectively with the needs of a changed (and still rapidly changing) world.

There are not many viable alternatives to the United Nations system, given: the fragmentation and political-economic crises in the former Soviet Union; Europe's preoccupation with both deepening and widening its Community integration; Japan's resistance to any increased military role, which is also widely opposed elsewhere in Asia; and -- not least -- the growing disinclination and inability of the United States to play world policeman, a role which in any case would not command international support. Many less-developed countries which already tend to see the UN Security Council as "the political arm of U.S. foreign policy"[1] would be even less inclined to accept a U.S. role as the world's "enforcer."

The need and opportunity to shape a more comprehensive security system through the United Nations is recognized, at least tacitly, by peoples and governments everywhere. This is confirmed by the astonishing number of new "peacekeeping" missions assigned to the UN in recent years. Many exceed the scope of "peacekeeping" as traditionally understood. That this would result from the demise of the Cold War and the collapse of the Soviet empire was by no means predictable.

The UN has so far met its new challenges with considerable success; but the real tests, in Cambodia, in Yugoslavia, and other regions facing destabilization, are yet to come. Whatever can be done organizationally, administratively and militarily -- to strengthen the UN's capacity to deal with them will help the UN to become a more reliable instrument for the maintenance or restoration of international peace and security.

It is said that the art of statesmanship is to turn what is into what ought to be. Given the rapid acceleration of the pace and magnitude of world change during the past few years, it is not easy to get a clear view of either the "is" or the "ought to be." For the world is in a major transitional phase comparable, in some ways, to post-World War II restructuring and decolonization. Harvard Professor Joseph Nye sees it also as a further erosion of the seventeenth century Westphalian system in which "order was based on the sovereignty of states, not the sovereignty of peoples." He and others demonstrate that it is by no means clear that the "New World Order" envisaged by President Bush after the victory in the Gulf, and before the fragmentation of the Soviet Union, can be realized or that it commands an international consensus.[2]

The world seems to be moving, rather like its own tectonic plates, in two contradictory directions simultaneously. Economically, the trend is toward integration into larger units -- as witnessed by the European Community, the projected North American Free Trade Area, and similar regional efforts elsewhere, such as in Latin America, even while GATT members struggle to complete the Uruguay Round of global trade liberalization.

Politically, however, the trend seems to be toward disintegration and fragmentation into smaller ethnic and nationality-based units, as seen in the former Soviet Union's new Commonwealth of Independent States, Yugoslavia, and Czechoslovakia. While these developments may be attributed to the end of the Communist empire, which long suppressed ethnic tensions, the phenomenon is also visible in the West. Even in Western Europe, the goal of political unity and federalism is proving far harder to achieve than economic union, as the negative Danish referendum of June 1992 showed. Canada periodically threatens to self-destruct over Quebec. Race problems plague the United States and some analysts see a tendency toward fragmentation into competing special interest groups at the expense of traditional notions of a common good or destiny, in effect an "ex uno plures."

Old regional and national groups are making new claims even in long established and democratic states such as the United Kingdom, France and Spain. In the Southern Hemisphere, Africa continues to suffer essentially tribal conflicts and civil wars, while India periodically endures eruptions of communal and separatist violence. Ethnic strife is no stranger to South East Asia; and it is endemic to the Middle East where it seems likely to persist even if progress is made on the fundamental Arab-Israeli conflict.

With the removal of the Cold War's rigidity and discipline and with the reduction in superpower client states and proxies, old intrastate conflicts are bound to surface. They may come to rival classical interstate acts of aggression as principal threats to international peace and security.

Separatist movements and even civil wars have traditionally been treated in international law generally and by the United Nations, as internal or domestic matters in which there is no international jurisdiction. The only exception is by invitation of the government concerned and with the concurrence of the contending parties, as in Yugoslavia in the early months of 1992.

Indeed, paragraph 7 of Article II of the UN Charter specifies that: "Nothing contained in the present Charter shall authorize the United Nations to intervene in matters which are essentially within the domestic jurisdiction of any state or shall require the members to submit such matters to settlement under the present Charter..."

There has therefore been a tendency to ignore even the most brutal activities of those tyrants that have aimed solely at their own people. The leaders of other countries, small and large, have feared that the precedent of UN action in such a case might return to plague them. The former Soviet Union was especially sensitive to alleged foreign or UN "interference" in its domestic affairs, but it was not alone. In fact, most less-developed countries have been zealous defenders of the principle of the inviolability of national sovereignty, and they have traditionally been joined en bloc, for obvious historic reasons, by the Latin American states. China has long held to its central principles of sovereign equality of states and non-interference in internal affairs.

Recently, however, this hostility to intervention by the international community even in cases of clear and widespread abuse of human rights has begun to erode. Haiti, where the UN was asked to supervise a free election (only to have the results overturned by a coup) is a recent example; and an even more current one is Somalia, where the UN is attempting to end a bloody civil war, despite the relatively limited international ramifications.

There is a clear connection between the current enthusiasm for democracy and an increased willingness to accept international intervention to redress the most flagrant violations of human rights. Likewise, there is a connection between the lack of democracy within a country and its tendency to commit such violations.[3] Indeed, returning to Article 2 (7) of the Charter, more and more attention is being paid to the final clause which reads: "...but this principle shall not prejudice the application of enforcement measures under Chapter VII."

A notable feature of the summit meeting of the Security Council in January 1992 was the explicit assertion by one participant, Hungary, of an international right of intervention to ensure respect for human rights, and the implicit endorsement of that principle by both Russia and the United Kingdom.[4] Subsequently, world opinion has focused on Serbian "aggression" against other former states of Yugoslavia and the resulting death, destruction, and flight of refugees. If diplomacy continues to fail, this will be the next area of UN "intervention."

If trends continue, the undertakings of States concerning not only human rights but the environment or control of nuclear materials seem likely to provide a basis for greater international jurisdiction.

The extent to which a "duty to intervene" on humanitarian or human rights grounds can establish itself as a valid basis for collective UN action remains to be seen. However, the Security Council has increasingly expanded the definition of what constitutes a "threat to international peace and security" in terms of enforcement action under Chapter VII. For example, Security Council Resolution 688 grants extraordinary authority for disarming Iraq and protecting minorities, although this was clearly a unique case stemming from that country's defeat in battle and acceptance of cease-fire conditions.

Large migrations of peoples and refugees across international borders and destabilization of those borders have occurred in many conflicts beside Iraq, such as the former Soviet Union and Yugoslavia, Somalia and elsewhere in East Africa and in Haiti. Some could be characterized as a threat to peace, depending on the circumstances.

Violations of the nuclear Non-Proliferation Treaty (NPT) would make an even better case for intervention. Indeed, the Union of Concerned Scientists has proposed that the UN Security Council appoint itself as the "principal enforcement arm" for the NPT if the safeguards and controls of the International Atomic Energy Agency (IAEA) fail.[5]

The problem of expanding UN jurisdiction, as some observers see it, is to develop objective criteria, such as the number of trans-border refugees or magnitude of civilian deaths and injuries from domestic hostilities. Although genocide is an international crime under the 1948 Convention on the

Prevention and Punishment of the Crime of Genocide (defined as acts committed with the "intent to destroy.... a national, ethnic, racial or religious group"), it does not cover political groupings nor does it explicitly authorize outside intervention.

Getting the United Nations to agree on a set of criteria is problematic -- whether in the Security Council, the General Assembly or, conceivably, the Economic and Social Council. It therefore seems desirable to seek advisory opinions from the International Court of Justice. Such opinions (which are provided for in the Charter) would be on whether a specific set of circumstances, including purely internal conflicts, anarchy and tyranny, would warrant intervention on humanitarian grounds.[6] The Court could draw not only on international conventions, such as human rights declarations and undertakings but also, as provided in Article 38 of the Court's Statute, on "international custom...the general principles of law recognized by civilized nations" and "judicial decisions and the teachings of the most highly qualified publicists of the various nations...." Such a procedure would treat international law as evolving and dynamic, and allow new international norms of behavior to be considered as they gain acceptance.

Based upon such an advisory opinion, the Security Council would find it easier to authorize enforcement actions either on humanitarian grounds alone or in the context of threats to international peace and security. Although the Council would not be required to act, such a procedure for obtaining prior judicial evaluation could restrain ill-considered or hasty responses. This could limit UN intervention to the most egregious cases which require an exception to the general rule that only States are the subjects of international law and are authoritative in matters of their municipal laws and domestic jurisdictions.

Questions of this type may soon provide more substance to future UN agendas than the aggression across international borders, which was the primary concern of the UN's founders and which has occurred in Korea, Israel, Iran, the Falklands, Kuwait, and elsewhere. The foregoing discussion suggests that the world will see a combination of military and non-military "threats" to the common "security" of UN members. Indeed, one leading expert on international law and organization, Columbia Professor Richard Gardner, suggests that "environment, population and drug trafficking are destined to be the three main non-military challenges to the U.S. and global security in the years ahead."[7]

It is difficult to see any military enforcement role for the United Nations in environmental or population matters. However, as noted above, human rights violations have already become a matter of significant international concern and in the views of some jurists and scholars, are evolving progressively into accepted norms of international law. There are precedents for economic and trade sanctions under UN auspices against such violations of human rights in Rhodesia-Zimbabwe, South Africa, and post-war Iraq; but there are few precedents thus far for military actions without the consent of the disputing parties to enforce human rights except in the special case of Iraq's Kurdish crisis.

Professor Gardner is surely right that the United Nations role will be expanding in those areas that transcend national boundaries, especially as peoples and governments perceive it as the only forum available for tackling global problems on the scale required. Economic development needs, e.g. for sustainable growth consistent with a viable human habitat, will gain a leading place on the world's agenda as military dangers recede. Many different components of the UN family such as the World Bank and International Monetary Fund, the UN International Development Organization (UNIDO), the Conference on Trade and Development (UNCTAD), the UN Environmental Program (UNEP), the Refugee Commission and the regional commissions will be even more involved. While we recognize the importance -- indeed, the urgency -- of some of these issues, they cannot be dealt with in the confines of this study.[8]

Peace and security missions fall into the broad categories set out by Chapter VI (peacemaking and peacekeeping) and Chapter VII's "Threats to the Peace, Breaches of the Peace, and Acts of Aggression." With the 1992 addition of Cambodia and Yugoslavia, the UN has mounted twenty-five peacekeeping operations since 1948. They are addressed in Chapter Four. The two cases of enforcement, namely Korea and Iraq, were described in the Overview as primarily U.S. operations with allied participation and UN approval. Even without any broadening of the UN's jurisdiction that may evolve, experience alone is sufficient to warrant an improved peace and security system of the type proposed in this book. In addition to the more traditional UN military activities, several other types of UN missions come to mind, some of them ancillary to other operations.

These possible future UN operations include:

• Protecting and extracting UN personnel, civilian or military, from a State or conflict which is endangering or mistreating them.

• Protection of unarmed micro states against coups organized by outside elements, as occurred in fact in the Maldive Islands in 1988.

• Suppression of the piracy which now preys on refugees in Southeast Asia, at the request of the governments concerned.

• Inhibiting or interdicting international trafficking in illegal drugs.

• Managing massive refugee migrations which exceed the control potential of states and other international organizations and providing emergency humanitarian aid in areas of natural or man-made disaster.

• Coordinating preemptive or punitive actions against either State-sponsored international terrorism or that of sub-national groups when INTERPOL, national intelligence or police resources are inadequate.

• Enforcing nuclear nonproliferation in coordination with or in support of the IAEA.

• Providing international intervention in unusual cases of human rights violations when the Security Council has determined to act, possibly based upon an advisory opinion by the International Court of Justice.

This list includes drug trafficking and anti-terrorism[9] as modern analogues to classical piracy along with one consequence of population explosions and civil strife, namely mass migrations of refugees which may overwhelm national authorities. It also includes possible enforcement of nonproliferation undertakings for nuclear weapons because of the implicit seriousness and the need to strengthen the existing international control regime. Other weapons of mass destruction, such as chemical and biological, might also come under international regimes via the treaties being negotiated. The dual use character and wide availability of key ingredients makes enforcement harder than in the nuclear weapons case.

The proliferation of conventional, and especially high technology, weapons is an increasing threat to international security. The UN General Assembly has therefore established a voluntary registry for arms production and transfers to provide greater transparency which, it is hoped, can exert some moderating influence through mutual self-restraint by the principal supplier countries. This is an area warranting a greater UN capacity for surveillance of international trouble spots and local arms races; but it must be omitted from the list of military enforcement possibilities, for the five permanent members of the Security Council are themselves the leading arms traffickers!

This overview of the UN's new environment presents more than enough likely scenarios calling for actual or potential employment of force to warrant a revision and extension of the UN peace and security system. In our view, it must include the capacity to apply timely, measured military force directly on behalf of the United Nations. The mere existence of such a capability can serve as a powerful deterrent and an inducement for hostile parties to settle differences by peaceful means. It is important to world stability and progress that the United Nations be perceived by the international community as a legitimate, if not indeed the primary, source of global "law and order," as well as a mediator.

Although the authors reached this conclusion after much consultation, we acknowledge that contrary views are held by some countries and more than a few experts on the United Nations.

Some simply fear that an effective United Nations peace and security system would lead to widening interventions in internal affairs and increased domination by the larger powers and the Security Council. Others believe that developing the UN's enforcement capabilities under Chapter VII will erode the organization's biggest asset, its ability to provide good offices without taking sides, and compromise traditional UN peacemaking and peacekeeping activities that require the consent of all parties.[10] Still others hold that despite Charter provisions to the contrary, the use of force by the UN contradicts the basic "principle of non-use of force except in self-defense...based on practical as well as idealistic considerations."[11]

In one sense, the issue evokes the U.S. Forest Service's policy of letting fires burn themselves out, while containing them within certain boundaries. Defenders of that policy say the forests will regenerate over time, as a natural phenomenon. By extension, some argue ethnic wars like the one in Yugoslavia should be allowed to burn out, to "exhaust their blood lust" as one U.S. official put it; and the international community should limit itself to humanitarian relief and containing the "fire."

Others consider such a policy morally indefensible when tens of thousands of innocent lives are at stake; and in any case, immediate media coverage may make it impossible for politicians to ignore devastation and suffering even in far-off places.

Such debates between pacifist and activist points of view, like theological disputes, cannot be settled logically. We believe that a stronger UN system would merely permit, rather than mandate, any commitment to military interventions. They must necessarily be decided on the merits of each individual case. A strengthened UN system would actually enhance prospects for peaceful resolutions by deterring certain forms of behavior.

Adapting the Security Council to New Circumstances

Another set of concerns about great power domination does require our reconsideration of the role and structure of the Security Council, since the UN Charter makes that body the final determinant in deciding "what measures shall be taken...to restore international peace and security" (Art. 39). All UN members "agree to accept and carry out the decisions" (Art. 25) of the Council; and every state accepts the obligation of the Charter as a condition of membership in the organization (Art.4).

The five permanent Council members: China, France, Russia (as the successor to the Soviet Union), the United Kingdom and the United States, are the victorious powers of World War II, and the world's declared nuclear powers. The ten non-permanent members (enlarged from six in 1965 by

Charter amendment) are elected by the General Assembly to two-year terms. In 1992 they are Austria, Belgium, Cape Verde, Ecuador, Hungary, India, Japan, Morocco, Venezuela and Zimbabwe.

The problem is that this structure does not reflect the realities of the contemporary world. It does not include on a continuing basis the economic superpowers, Germany and Japan, or the largest regional powers such as India, Brazil or Nigeria, or relatively wealthy countries like Canada and Italy. Nor does it fully reflect the availability of military power for United Nations purposes.

This unrepresentative character of the permanent membership tends to reinforce concerns about the Council's "great power chauvinism." We believe that a more acceptable Security Council structure is a sine qua non of the enhanced peace and security system we are proposing.

If a United Nations were being created today without reference to World War II, international power might be conceived as a combination of population and geography, economic strength, military assets and potential, and such intangibles as the moral credibility of democracy, leadership and responsibility.

In geographic terms, seven countries exceed (and only three others even approach) 1 million square miles of territory, which equals about 1.7% of the world's land surface. Size alone would nominate Russia, China, the U.S.A., Canada, Brazil, India, and Argentina. Population, as listed in Table I (in Appendix B), would nominate (in order): China, India, the U.S., Indonesia, Brazil, Russia, Japan, Pakistan, Bangladesh, Nigeria, Mexico and Germany as over 80 million people.

If we take GNP as a proxy for economic strength, recognizing that many other elements are involved, and use 300 billion (U.S.) dollars[12] as a cutoff point, the rankings in Table II would nominate: the U.S., Japan, Russia, Germany, France, Italy, the U.K., Canada, Ukraine, China, Brazil, Spain and India.

Countries on both the population and GNP list include only three of the five permanent members (U.S., Russia and China, but not France and U.K.), plus Japan, Germany, Brazil, and India. With regard to the military dimension, all five permanent members are nuclear weapons states; and all have substantial military forces with some power projection capability, as do the four other "dual list" countries. As for the others, Canada, Italy, and perhaps one or two others, such as Ukraine or, on a regional basis Nigeria or Egypt, might be added. Each could manage a few battalions without mobilizing reserves.[13]

The point is that under such objective criteria only about a dozen of the world's 175 UN members would qualify for special consideration to be members of an augmented Security Council structure.

Obstacles to Change

Any adjustments to the formal membership of the Security Council would, of course, require further amendment to the Charter under Chapter XVIII, which must be approved by two-thirds of the membership, including all permanent members of the Security Council, who therefore have the power of veto. Britain and France would almost certainly veto any amendment which would eliminate their Council membership. Conceivably, if and as the European Community develops a single foreign and defense structure, a "European" seat or even two could be created; but that lies far in the future. It might also open the door to claims from the Commonwealth of Independent States, the Arab League, the OAS and other groupings.

Simply adding "permanent members" may paralyze the Security Council by the proliferation of veto power. Moreover, such additions without also adding to the rotational or elected members would probably be unacceptable to the General Assembly. If both categories were enlarged, the Council would become so unwieldy as to be incapable of producing a working majority in favor of enforcement actions. Even at its present size of fifteen, Security Council support of the coalition against Iraq was held together only with difficult negotiations, arm-twisting (including financial inducements) and diplomatic maneuvering. So any changes must provide for the maintenance and if possible, enhancement of the Council's present capacity for cohesive action.

One approach would be to establish a second tier of five "alternating seats" between the permanent and elected members. Thus key regional countries might be paired, for example: (1) Europe: Germany and Italy, (2) South Asia: India and Pakistan/Indonesia, (3) Pacific: Japan and the Republic of Korea, (4) Latin America: Brazil and Argentina/Mexico, and (5) Africa:

Nigeria and Egypt.* Only one would serve at a time, rotating annually or in two year cycles, but the potentially most helpful regional powers would thus be permanently drawn into the work of the Security Council. The representation of developing countries would be far stronger in the Council's deliberations because they would no longer be competing with the "alternating Member States." Without necessarily diluting its effectiveness, the smaller regional powers would have a greater opportunity to be selected to the existing ten rotational seats. The Council would then have twenty instead of fifteen members, which is probably the outside limit of manageability. The ten-plus alternating countries would have to be kept up to speed on Council activities through UN and regional consultations so that each would be ready to take its place in the Security Council and also participate in security activities with desirable consistency.

A somewhat analogous system was devised to solve the Nuclear Planning Group membership dilemma at NATO in the 1960's: all Alliance members except France and Iceland joined a Nuclear Defense Affairs Committee (NDAC) which served as an umbrella for the smaller and more operational Nuclear Planning Group, which originally had both permanent and rotational members from the NDAC.

There are good arguments for avoiding any amendments to the UN Charter, since the process could open a Pandora's box of uncertainty. Some members fear losing important existing provisions, while others would doubtless propose major changes which might prove undesirable, such as eliminating the veto in the Security Council altogether. Our recommendation, therefore, is to proceed without Charter amendments at the present time along both of the following lines: First, if the cooperation of the General Assembly and its key regional caucuses can be obtained, to encourage the regular election of the five "alternating members" to the Council from among a predetermined list of major regional states which are not permanent members. (However, unless the total was increased (via Charter amendment) the opportunities for smaller states to serve would be reduced.)

Second, use the authority of Article 29, which allows the Council to establish "such subsidiary organs as it deems necessary," to establish a <u>Peace</u>

---

* Canada and a member of the Nordic countries might also be included in this scheme because of their outstanding contributions to UN peacekeeping.

Management Committee made up of the permanent Council members, the augmentation of the ten-plus countries listed above, and other members that were contributing substantially to UN peacekeeping and peace enforcement, such as by earmarking units for the proposed Quick Reaction Force (QRF). This conforms to the intent of Article 44 which provides access to the Council for countries contributing forces to UN operations.

Under this procedure, whereby the Committee recommendations would be acted upon by the Council, the smaller rotational members would still have their rights as Council members, even though they would not be participants in the work of the Committee. Its total membership would almost certainly be less than 20 but it would be far more representative of the real world power structure than the present Council alone. Appointment to the Peace Management Committee would be by the Council on the recommendation of the Secretary-General but based upon the objective criteria discussed above, such as contributing or earmarking substantial (at least a brigade or equivalent) military forces for the United Nations.

In acting on the advice and recommendations of the Committee, the Council would retain its Charter responsibilities and could act only upon the affirmative vote of nine members, as at present. Permanent members might also pledge not to exercise their veto, unless supported by at least one other country, except in cases of "extreme national interest."

Appointment to the Peace Management Committee -- which could help the Secretary-General manage peacekeeping and enforcement operations should be limited to the states fulfilling the criteria of being a major regional or global power and a contributor of substantial forces to the UN's QRF, as determined in a recommendation of the Secretary-General.

We believe that the committee approach could succeed; it would assure the participation of major regional powers and rectify the most glaring omissions. Analogous proposals have already been made: for example, Japanese Prime Minister Miyazawa suggested to the Security Council Summit of January 31, 1992 "a consultative group of an appropriate size whose members would include countries which were major contributors of funds, among other things, as well as the countries concerned in the region."[14] However, we propose a Standing Committee, not ad hoc groupings, and the Committee would, when required, invite countries furnishing major forces to an operation, to participate in decisions and recommendations to the Security

Council as provided for in Articles 31 and 44.

Is the UN Willing to Change?

In a 1991 communication to members, the United Nations Association of the U.S.A. commented that none of the national leaders hailing a new world order "has attached to this vision a call for a framework of international law or institutions, or even for adapting existing UN machinery to new tasks...," suggesting, said the U.N.A.-U.S.A., "the reluctance of major powers to entrust actual enforcement responsibilities to the UN...". By the end of the year that situation had changed, at least to the extent that the major powers, and most UN member states, now recognize the need for a major re-organization of the UN's administrative machinery.

The new Secretary-General, Boutros-Ghali, took office on the understanding that he would initiate such an overhaul, and at the end of the summit meeting of the Security Council on 31 January 1992, the Council invited him to submit, by 1 July 1992, "his analysis and recommendations on ways of strengthening and making more efficient, within the framework and provisions of the Charter, the capacity of the United Nations for preventive diplomacy, for peacemaking and for peacekeeping," including recommendations on "ways of making more effective Secretariat planning and operations."[15]

In response to that mandate, the Secretary-General issued the June 17th report on "An Agenda for Peace" already noted. Although falling short of the recommendations in this book, it goes further than any other UN document of similar scope in recent memory, according to one long-time UN watcher. It presents a vision for the future and a comprehensive approach to global peace and security, in which the UN would have a "wider mission."

In addition, Boutros-Ghali had earlier announced, as a first stage in the administrative re-organization of the UN, the appointment of three principal Under-Secretaries, the reduction of the number of Deputy-Secretaries from 20 to 8, and some centralization of peacekeeping functions. Currently, Vladimir Petrovsky (a Russian) handles political affairs, disarmament and some peacekeeping; James Jonah of Sierra Leone handles African and Near Eastern peacekeeping; and Marrack Goulding of the United Kingdom heads a department of peacekeeping operations.

Although these actions represent, on paper at least, a significant step towards simplifying and centralizing the Secretariat's chains of command, much remains to be done. To summarize, the structure of the United Nations remains inadequate to operate a strengthened "peace and security system" even if the larger countries and other members agreed to establish it. The entire machine needs further overhaul, streamlining, and restructuring, which is addressed below in Chapter Three.

The old East-West fracture line which paralyzed the UN during the Cold War is now healing, bringing a reduced relevance to the so-called non-aligned movement. But the other fracture line between the wealthy, industrialized "North" and the developing and generally impoverished "South" can be expected to widen in the post-Cold War era. (The June 1992 Rio de Janeiro Conference on the Environment and Development illustrated the potential for rich-poor discord.)

At times the General Assembly and some specialized agencies, such as UNESCO, have been as paralyzed by the split between the Group of 77 (now composed of over 130 developing countries) and the OECD industrialized group as the Security Council was by the Cold War. For example, endless battles over proposed "codes of conduct" for multinational enterprises took up hundreds of man-years in several UN forums, often with little result. The growing phenomenon of business transnationalism was opposed by some on ideological, anti-business grounds while others sought to turn it into a vehicle for resource and technology transfer, free or on favorable terms, from North to South.[16]

Like any international organization, the UN can only do what its now 175 member countries can agree to; first by voting and ultimately by individually doing or paying for. The member governments are often of very different minds as to both ends and means. Some long-time observers divide the members into the major, "middle" or regional powers, and smaller countries. Each grouping has a few consistently responsible members who take the larger vision of the world body and contribute disproportionally to it, such as the Scandinavians and Canadians and at times the Egyptians and Indians. Others, like the former Soviet Union and its allies, had mostly been obstructionist. Most members probably see the UN in a parochial light and seek to block any actions which could harm their policy agendas, such as territorial claims or acquiring advanced military technologies. At the same time they pursue all possible direct benefits from aid programs, key staff positions, and "pork barrel" projects, such as regional offices and conferences.

Some countries energetically use the UN as a vehicle for their policy objectives -- the United States among them, while others treat it essentially as a side show, or a forum for scoring debating points or caucusing with like-minded delegates. As one former UN official wrote to the authors, "We have not gotten past the period when national sovereignty, skeletons in the cupboard and other traumas rule the passions and policies of virtually all governments."

On the other hand the cooperation and dissolution of the Soviet Union into a new Russia and fourteen other members, the staying power of the Arabian/Persian Gulf coalition, and the new effectiveness of the Security Council, particularly with the U.S.-led military forces, may have had a re-invigorating effect on the UN system, as Thomas Pickering, former U.S. Ambassador to the U.N., has argued persuasively.[17] The agreement of the bickering parties and the UN that the organization would actually run the interim government in Cambodia is unprecedented. It is a major, $2 billion-plus undertaking which will stretch the its capacity and may outrun its budget. The Europeans needed to turn to the UN and the Security Council to assume the responsibility and authority for operations regarding the dissolution of Yugoslavia. That too will be an operation of an unprecedented scale.

To a larger extent than in most intergovernmental organizations, the leadership and consensus building abilities of the Secretary-General and his deputies determine the UN's effectiveness. This has been true since the days of activists Trygve Lie and Dag Hammerskjold through the more cautious incumbencies of U Thant, Kurt Waldheim, and, until his triumphal grand finale, Perez de Cuellar.*

The Ambassadorial representatives of the members to the UN also vary widely in commitment, outlook, energy and abilities. These personal characteristics enable some individuals to play a consensus-building and

---

* The selection of Egyptian Deputy Prime Minister for foreign affairs, Boutros-Ghali, as successor to Javier Perez de Cuellar is symbolic not only of change, but of the UN's Byzantine politics of blocs. The selection process has been compared to "three dimensional chess;" in this case, avoiding a French veto of non-Francophones while pitting Arab Africa against sub-Saharans who had a candidate from Zimbabwe. (The Permanent Five did not have a firm contender of their own.) Despite the process, the UN appears to have made a fortunate selection. (See also endnote #18.)

leadership role which is disproportionate to the actual size or influence of the country represented. Others can and have exerted their influence negatively. Some have considerable stature with their own government, which is important if they are to "lobby" for UN budgets and programs at home, while others are not well connected at home, but enjoy a high standing in UN circles. Only a few have both, and some have neither.

Outsiders concerned with developing the new potential of the UN can only hope for the success of a "reform caucus for effectiveness," which is already networking within the UN system to build consensus among such key players as Secretariat officials, national representatives, leaders in home governments, and nongovernmental organizations. The NGOs, for example, the United Nations Association of the U.S.A. or the NGO Committee on Disarmament can be particularly effective in educating and mobilizing world opinion about the need for the UN to meet (and pay for) its new challenges.

Will Countries Adapt?

For the UN to fulfill its wider mission, there will have to be two basic changes. One concerns its capacity to operate major military forces as developed elsewhere in this book. The other depends on the attitude of the member countries and particularly those represented on the Security Council -- not least the United States -- toward the UN institution as an instrument of peace under law. The two are obviously interrelated, for confidence in the UN is related to its capacity. And that capacity can only be provided by those members who have enough confidence to give it a chance.

France and Britain, no longer global powers, have always seen the UN as a source of stability in the less developed world and have been active peacekeeping participants. At the January 1992 summit Security Council meeting, French President Mitterand offered 1,000 men to the UN on 48 hours notice, to be doubled within a week.[19] Britain and France together made up 15% of the total UN forces deployed at the end of 1991.

Communist China has been at best a silent partner since the People's Republic succeeded Taiwan in "China's seat" on the Council. But it does have a team in Iraq as part of the "Provide Comfort" operations, marking the first time all five permanent members have ever acted together! At the UN Security Council summit, China disappointingly spoke mainly to its traditional five principles, including noninterference in internal affairs and the sovereign equality of states.

The Soviet Union, once entirely negative, is succeeded by a Russia which shows every sign of wanting to play a positive and active role -- and which has surplus military manpower and assets seeking a mission. President Yeltsin told the Security Council that "We need a special rapid-response mechanism...and [we] are prepared to play a practical role in United Nations peacekeeping operations and contribute to their logistical support." Subsequently, Russian troops have in fact become part of the UN operations in Yugoslavia, another "first" if one excludes the special Kurdish protection operation in Iraq. Ukrainian units are also taking part. Russian Foreign Minister Andrei Kozyrev wrote in the Spring 1992 Foreign Affairs that Russia: "intends to promote in every possible way the strengthening of the United Nations...and increase the efficiency of UN activities...[working] actively on the issues of UN reform."

The United States, however, has been more of a verbal and political supporter of UN peacekeeping. It has never given military support to UN operations a high priority in sharp contrast to NATO requirements which have dominated Pentagon defense planning. Not only is the U.S. still paying off some $700 million of arrears owed the UN, but of the 11,209 military personnel serving in eleven peacekeeping operations at the end of 1991, only 88 (less than 1%) were American. Of the nearly 800 fatalities in 43 years of such operations, only 10 were American. In fairness, however, both superpowers were almost automatically excluded from peacekeeping missions during the Cold War. Moreover, we are here referring to peacekeeping operations, not enforcement, such as in Korea and Kuwait.

More importantly, the U.S. still seems guided by its Cold War distrust of "Communist" and former Communist countries, by its belief that, as a superpower, its own security does not depend on the UN, and by an unwillingness to have U.S. forces serving under foreign command. In other words, unless the U.S. calls the shots and commands the forces, it may be unwilling to play. There is also a lingering distrust of the United Nations and its international bureaucracy, notwithstanding several recent successes, including the end of the hostage crisis.

It is not mere oversight that Washington's initial planning for its post-Cold War military structure placed little or no emphasis on supporting multinational peacekeeping. Only one of the Pentagon's seven scenarios for "planning guidance" reported in the press[20] envisaged allied participation, and that is the highly unlikely case of a NATO counterattack against a Russian invasion of Poland and Lithuania. Nor does the parallel work undertaken in Congress, such as by House Armed Forces Committee Chairman Les Aspin,[21] envision a U.S. role in UN peacemaking. These lacunae at once understate potential requirements for many possible "threats to the peace" and overstate them: by suggesting that the United States will go it alone -- if it goes at all!

That assumption is highly questionable, for we have seen that neither American nor world opinion seems likely to tolerate the United States as the world cop on the block. On the other hand, as the cases of Iraq and Yugoslavia suggest, active U.S. leadership remains a sine qua non of effective international action.

To be sure, the U.S. must retain the force structure and reconstitution capacity to meet its own vital security interests, without having to rely on others who might not, in the event, be willing or able to help. But to restructure our forces with little reference to UN contingencies or the potential contributions of others through the UN seems inconsistent with the new world order and international security era that United States officials have proclaimed! At the least, it illustrates the mind-set in official Washington which will have to be adjusted before revitalized UN peacekeeping and common enforcement can become a reality.

Happily, initial Pentagon planning guidance was revised under pressure of foreign and domestic criticism to reflect a better balance between unilateral and collective security approaches, e.g. a "network of interlocking institutions" including NATO, and, presumably the United Nations, as well as other alliances. The new guidance also downplays the earlier emphasis on preventing the "reemergence of a new rival" which could pose a threat to U.S. interests. National Security Advisor Brent Scowcroft made the reference to the UN explicit as a central element of collective security in his remarks to the Eisenhower Institute award dinner on June 5, 1992.[22]

Still another factor complicates the emergence of big power confidence in the UN: the competing designs of France and Germany and of Britain and the United States for a security structure covering Europe or the "Euro-Atlantic Community." The first two countries, with some support from other

European Community members, seek a "European" force, currently embodied in a planned 35,000 man joint army corps, building on an existing but only partially operational Franco-German brigade, to be available in 1995. The U.S. and Britain, by contrast, stress the vital role of NATO in stabilizing European security. The French want the "Eurocorps" to "reinforce" NATO (to which its own forces have not been assigned since the days of General de Gaulle) but to be available for peacekeeping missions elsewhere. Germany insists that its forces can only be deployed under NATO, at least until its constitutional constraints are changed.[23]

Meanwhile the NATO Foreign Ministers formally agreed that, notwithstanding its traditional reluctance to engage in "out of area" activities, NATO assets henceforth could be used in peacekeeping in Europe.[24] Beyond that the North Atlantic Cooperation Council (NACC), an informal grouping of NATO and former Warsaw Pact members, has discussed joint peacekeeping, perhaps under the umbrella of the Conference on Security and Cooperation in Europe (CSCE). Conspicuously absent, until now, has been detailed consideration of peacekeeping (or enforcement) by European military elements under direct United Nations auspices. The Yugoslavian problems may see a reversal of that reluctance.

The goal of French policy has long been to maximize French leverage by emphasizing forums which do not include the U.S., and their jockeying for position is muddying the overall picture. Ironically, the one case where military intervention is currently needed, Yugoslavia, so far represents a failure of European diplomacy.[25] It has had to be referred to the Security Council for sanctions, while possible military contributions were debated in a European-NATO-CSCE context.

On paper, the solution is obvious: have the CSCE formally declared a UN regional security body whose enforcement actions must be approved by the Security Council under Article 53, but let the actual forces be provided by the NACC, NATO, the Western European Union (WEU), the Eurocorps, or their cooperating members as circumstances dictate. In part, the reluctance to take this step reflects the competing agendas of key countries; but it is also a manifestation of lack of confidence in the UN and a reluctance to admit non-Atlantic voices into European security debates.

It is obvious then that the vicious circle of no confidence without capacity and little capacity without more confidence can be broken only if work on both elements proceeds in parallel: entrusting the UN with greater operational tasks, while simultaneously enhancing its capabilities along the lines proposed in the succeeding chapters.

No one would suggest that major countries should entirely entrust their security entirely to even an effective and pro-active United Nations. The composition of the Security Council and the possibility of a veto would make this unacceptable. Moreover, a national military establishment has always been the hallmark of sovereignty. We do suggest, however, that in a period of sharply lowered threat perceptions, an effective United Nations security structure, motivated and equipped to play a more active role, would increase international trust, confidence and security. That, in turn, should encourage patterns of collective security cooperation and permit the gradual reduction of armaments and forces that exceed basic security needs of nations.

CHAPTER TWO

MILITARY FORCES FOR UN OPERATIONS

The UN's Requirements For Military Forces

In coming years, the military forces and resources that the UN may need for its various tasks could run the entire military gamut. The end of the Cold War and the consequent unblocking of the Security Council have made it possible for the world's governments, acting under the UN Charter, to undertake more and broader UN actions having military aspects, and the recent flood of regional disputes has enlarged the need for such services.

The requirements will surely include further "peacekeeping" deployment of forces with the consent of the disputing parties under Chapter VI. The purpose is to assist the disputants in pacific settlement of their differences and provide neutral good offices. It is also possible to foresee the necessity for a variety of "enforcement" operations, i.e., actions of a deterrent or coercive nature under Chapter VII, taken without the consent of both parties, to counter a threat to the peace, to suppress aggression or to deal with breaches of the peace.[1]

At the lower limit, some of the calls on the UN, such as observation, information gathering, reconnaissance, liaison, or "good offices" or mediation missions can be handled by individuals or small groups. Sometimes, however, the need is for organized units, from relatively small ones to very substantial formations. Operations Desert Shield and Desert Storm required land, sea, and air elements able to fight large scale war. Peacekeeping forces now deployed in Cambodia and the former Yugoslavia, while not designed for major combat, require large numbers, many skills, and much equipment.

Given the uncertainties of nuclear proliferation, it is not inconceivable that at some point early in the next century, the United Nations might be forced to deal with an aggressor armed with nuclear weapons or with cases of nuclear blackmail. With all permanent members of the Security Council being major nuclear powers, action to deter or counter such a threat would have to be taken by one or more of them on behalf of the UN as a whole, as we do not envisage any of the UN forces we are discussing in this book as possessing or requiring nuclear weapons of any type.

However, the question of a *defense* against limited missile attacks which might involve nuclear warheads has already arisen in proposals for a modified Strategic Defense Initiative (SDI) or Global Protection Against Limited Strikes (GPALS). If the threat requires and available technology permits, such a system might conceivably be deployed under UN Security Council auspices, perhaps through several national executive agents, as a better alternative than U.S.-Russian, or even NATO sponsorship.[2]

Returning to conventional military forces, the nature of those needed will be different in the changing situations. In most cases, peacekeeping forces are lightly armed for self-defense. Normally, they do not need massive armaments, the backup to support combat nor the replenishment of battle expenditures and combat losses. Their essentials are adequate numbers of well-trained men,* mobility, good local and global communications and intelligence support, reasonable amenities, and adequate logistics. Frequently, constabulary elements make valuable contributions. Peacekeepers need specialized training for their role; the "Soldiers Without Enemies" mission is quite different from that of a fighting force and should be well understood by the troops before they arrive in the theater.

Enforcement missions, on the other hand, must have, on a scale appropriate to the opposition, a full panoply of people, arms, and support, trained and tuned for combat. The boundary between the nature of the forces required for peacekeeping and enforcement, however, is not absolute.

---

* Some peacekeeping forces from Scandinavian countries have included women as members of their national contributions, to which there has been no objection. However, as far as international forces, such as the UN Legion, are concerned, we do not feel it appropriate to add the gender dimension to the already difficult task of integrating many races, cultures, nationalities and religions into an effective unit, especially one designed for combat roles. When and if women are generally accepted in the combat arms of most UN Security Council members, the question can and should be considered.

Peacekeepers must always be able to fight in self-defense, and should be alert to and prepared for the possibility of broader combat action if a situation changes -- say, by the withdrawal of consent by one party. And combat-capable backup should be planned and kept at appropriate readiness for engaged peacekeeping forces when the threat of hostile action justifies.

For both peacekeeping and enforcement, the UN operational forces and field headquarters must be tailored to the demands of the specific situation; each mission has its own problems and its requirements, and both change with the dynamics of the situation.

The duration of the UN's need for presence and forces also varies widely in different cases. Of the 25 peacekeeping operations initiated from 1948 to the present -- 15 being observer missions and 10 with peacekeeping forces -- 11 are still in commission, including two established in the 1940's. The remainder endured for periods of six months to 11 years. As for enforcement operations, while Desert Storm as such is essentially over, the UN Command in Korea is still nominally functioning after four decades. In all the long-lasting operations, of course, rotation of personnel keeps the duration of individual assignment within reasonable limits, but the load on the UN remains.

The number and scope of UN military operations in the coming years cannot be predicted. It appears, however, that the world will continue to be profoundly unsettled. It is torn with regional, international, ethnic, and ideological hostilities. It has lost the discipline that the Cold War imposed on the entire globe. Further, the performance of the UN in a succession of recent incidents has enhanced its reputation and the likelihood of its being called upon. There is, moreover, a widespread preference for using international rather than national responses to threats to peace.

In recent months the UN has called up over 30,000 consensual military peacekeepers, in addition to those already assigned to ongoing UN operations. It seems probable that the demand for UN peacekeeping forces will continue and grow.

If the UN is to become the effective mechanism for maintaining international peace that was its founders' vision, the organization will need combat forces capable of enforcement operations. When faced by the threats to the peace, breaches of the peace, or acts of aggression covered by Chapter VII, the non-military measures of its Article 41 will be given redoubled force by the existence of an evident <u>potential</u> UN combat ability. And situations that demand <u>actual</u> military operations under Article 42 are surely to be expected, sooner or later, whether in a deterrent mode or in combat actions.

The classic enforcement task, meeting aggression across an international boundary, is not obsolete, as Desert Shield/Storm demonstrated and as many conceivable contingencies could require -- for a current, not unthinkable example, the undertaking of the defense of UN Members Croatia and Bosnia-Herzegovina against Serbian invasion. Short of an actual invasion, states could be given UN deterrent support in defending their frontiers against hostile neighbors, as Desert Shield/Storm was first assigned to support the defense of Saudi Arabia. A peacekeeping operation could be transformed into an enforcement one by hostile actions of one side or the other, as may well occur in Cambodia or the former Yugoslavia. Moreover, as discussed in Chapter One, there are growing calls within the UN for international or humanitarian intervention in cases of egregious violations of human rights by a government against its own people. Conventional operations, such as air strikes, might have to be employed to enforce nuclear nonproliferation undertakings analogous to Israel's unilateral action against Iraq in 1981, or to support by force IAEA or treaty inspections of nuclear facilities which an obligated country refused to permit. Such a scenario appears to be unfolding in Iraq as this book goes to press. Force under the UN might have to be brought to bear on "low intensity" and increasingly challenging international issues such as: terrorism; piracy; protecting refugees; restoring order where anarchy prevails; securing ports, airheads, or supply lines for humanitarian or security reasons; rescuing attacked or captured peacekeepers, diplomats, or others. Enforcement, therefore, in a wide range of types and intensities could become a more and more demanding concern of the UN.

The UN's military capabilities for all these widely varying roles, cannot be met by a simple structure planned and acquired in advance of demand. Of course, the UN can and should improve its ability to anticipate problems. While the needs and options that have continued year after year are reasonably predictable, in this volatile world it would be visionary to expect the Security Council and the budget-approving General Assembly to foresee all of the UN's requirements with enough precision to justify acquiring large UN forces in advance.

It is conceivable that in the very long term the UN might create large international forces of its own, able to assume much of the task of maintaining global peace and thus to relieve individual nations of some or all of their own force requirements, but that solution is at best far distant. In the meantime, the UN can maintain a small standing force sufficient for low intensity operations and some of the more predictable types of contingencies. Only if such efforts prove successful, and in the light of experience gained should the UN move on to more ambitious efforts.

It follows that, for the present and foreseeable future, the UN's operational military forces must be built case-by-case as new requirements develop and as operations end or change their scope. The UN must continue to rely on the member nations to provide the needed forces from their national military establishments on the UN's call, as and when they are needed. And for that, a comprehensive system must be developed to replace ad hoc improvisation. For such on-call forces to be able to operate effectively together, the UN will have to provide the supplying nations current guidance for training, equipping and indoctrinating their forces for coordinated UN action. Joint command, staff and force exercises would be highly desirable.

The UN does need some standing military elements. In particular, the UN Headquarters at present lacks a satisfactory military staff for the anticipation of challenges and threats, for strategic and force planning, for the operation and logistical support of peacekeeping and enforcement forces. The Security Council and Secretary-General need an adequate military staff which is professionally competent and positioned so as to make its contribution effective to and through the Secretary-General. Additionally, a standing military formation of modest size, a UN Legion, which is immediately responsive to UN command and control, would be uniquely useful and fully justified in order to cope with a number of present and foreseeable circumstances.

The standing elements, UN Military Staff and UN Legion, would be made up of individuals -- as distinct from organized national units -- who have volunteered to be seconded from the armed forces of many member nations.[3] Its members should be required to conform to the Charter requirements and staff rules that apply to civilian elements of the Secretariat, including: "not seek nor receive instructions from any government or from any other authority external to the Organization" and "refrain from any action which might reflect on their position as international officials responsible to the Organization."

Both the Military Staff and Legion would thus be entirely international, with organizational loyalty only to the UN while in its service. Their functioning should therefore be free, and be seen to be free, of regional, national, or ethnic bias. Such impartiality would be an essential element of their effectiveness.

In sum, to meet its military requirements for peacekeeping and enforcement, the UN needs to be able to acquire from members all types of military forces, from seconded individuals to small to large military units, volunteered from the armed forces of member nations for short or long periods, in numbers which are not predictable; it needs a military command and control system to guide combined preparation of these forces and to direct them in a wide range of operations; and its capabilities would be greatly enhanced by having the flexibility, readiness and example of a standing international UN Legion of modest size. At the least, such a force should be initiated on an experimental basis.

Providing and Directing the UN's Military Forces

The Executive Agent

The UN system for military enforcement is embodied in Chapter VII of the Charter. It has never been actually used. The UN system for military aspects of peacekeeping under Chapter VI was not foreseen in the Charter, but has been developed over the years through practical experience. The stipulated enforcement system is probably unworkable without adaptation and development. The military aspects of peacekeeping could be built upon and substantially improved. The enhanced system should serve both peacekeeping and enforcement.

In the divided Security Council of the Cold War years, any truly United Nations directed enforcement was impossible. In the only events where enforcement with a UN authorization was undertaken, Korea and Desert Storm, UN military direction and control were nominal. The Security Council gave no strategic directives; it raised no objection to national or coalition action; in Korea it was scarcely informed. The U.S., not the UN, actually and visibly directed the operations. The Military Staff Committee atrophied.

Even with the Security Council functioning proactively, the Charter concept must be further developed in order to carry out truly UN-directed enforcement operations. The original concept under the Charter was for the Security Council to agree on high strategy as did the World War II summit conferences, for the Military Staff Committee to exercise strategic direction as did the WWII Combined Chiefs of Staff, and for a theater commander in the field to carry out the operation. More specifically, the Charter calls for the Security Council, assisted by the Military Staff Committee, to make plans for the application of armed force and to direct the employment and command of UN forces.

It is possible for broad directives for planning and operations to be drafted and agreed upon by international committees like the Council and the Staff Committee (if the latter were resurrected) and such directives should be the authority for and specify the scope of peacemaking and enforcement action as the Charter contemplates. But for the implementation of such committee directives, including the detailed planning for, and direction of, forces in conformity with those directives, a committee is not suitable; an implementing single executive is essential. This at once became evident when the UN began to develop the peacekeeping system through practical experience with actual missions. The peacekeeping system as developed provides, in essence, that the Security Council authorize a peacekeeping operation, prescribe its mission, scope, and financing, and ask the Secretary-General to carry it out. The Secretary-General, functioning within the Security Council's authorization, is the actual executive and directs the field commanders, civil and military.

The need for an executive is even more urgent in enforcement, where the requirement is to direct the preparation, execution, and support of threatened or actual combat, and it seems clear that for enforcement as well as peacekeeping the executive should be the Secretary-General. The Charter, by implication, leaves the executive assignment for enforcement to the field commander. That solution fails to take account of the intermingling of political and military elements in the executive task -- at the UN and with the highest levels of member governments -- which cannot be managed by a military field headquarters. It also does not recognize the need for the executive to handle and coordinate a number of simultaneous missions with different field commanders, or the fact that important elements of the executive task must be accomplished before the field commander is designated and ready to function and may last well after his disestablishment. The field commander, or commanders, will in any case be more than occupied in conducting the military operations on the scene.

It is the Secretary-General who has the continuity, the international stature, and the close association with the Security Council needed for the executive role, and he directs the Secretariat, where the additional civil and military resources needed for effective executive control can be located efficiently. Most important, he is an international servant; his actions are impartial and are recognized as such.

In some situations the Secretary-General may not be a workable choice for executive. He may be simply overloaded by the number and scope of operations undertaken at the same time, or by an operation of such magnitude and complexity that it is beyond the capacity of his then-existing staff to handle. Operations undertaken by or with the "Regional Arrangements" covered in Chapter VIII of the Charter or with a nation or consortium of nations that the Security Council decides to support may require the selection of the leader of one of the involved parties. In any of these cases, the Security Council could designate as its executive a chief of state or of an alliance (assuming he had adequate staff and military resources for the task), while maintaining over-arching UN control by specifying the mission, scope, objective, and limits of the executive assignment. Even in cases of such delegation as a last resort, if the Security Council is to discharge its responsibilities for oversight, the Secretary-General and his staff should play a prominent role as the eyes and ears of the Council, to insure that the Council is amply informed for decision-making, that the Council's directives are in fact being followed by the executive, and that the reality of UN control is diluted as little as possible.

The Secretary-General, then, should organize as the executive agent of the Security Council for both peacemaking and enforcement, in such a way as to be able to anticipate needs for UN action and, when the Council directs action, to be able to evaluate the consequent requirements, find the resources, put together the forces, designate and staff the commanders, and direct and support the operations.

The United Nations Military Staff

To be able to discharge these functions for both peacekeeping and enforcement, the Secretary-General must have as an element of his organization a competent and ample UN Military Staff.

The Military Staff should be led by a very senior Chief, an officer of international reputation and sufficient stature to deal effectively with military and civilian leaders at the UN and around the world. The Chief of Staff would be appointed by the Secretary-General with the informal concurrence of the Council. He would report to the Secretary-General directly and through the appropriate Deputy Secretary-General. He might sit with, though not be accountable to, any reactivated Military Staff Committee, serving as that body's liaison with the Secretary-General. He would be the senior military officer in the UN chain of command to its assigned military forces, and consequently the commander to whom the military forces in UN service would report, subject of course to the broader authority and responsibility of the Secretary-General.

The UN Military Staff would be made up of individuals appointed by the Chief of Staff from the military establishments of member nations. They would require seconding from their government to the UN Secretariat. They would wear the uniform of the UN and be equipped with the material essential for effective planning, operations and communication. The Military Staff would number at least 200 officers, in contrast to the half-dozen now on the Secretary-General's staff.

Some have recommended that the Military Staff be established in the Military Staff Committee (MSC). It may be that reviving the MSC and providing it with some staffing could assist the Security Council in formulating its overall directives for peacemaking and enforcement, perhaps providing more direct continuing input from the military headquarters of the permanent members. But the organizational site where a substantial working UN Military Staff is essential is in the Secretariat, where the Secretary-General is faced with actually directing military forces and operations. As noted above, there are sharp limits on how much a committee can accomplish even in a quasi-executive capacity, and there are other reasons for limiting the MSC's role. Developments in political-military coordination since the Charter was written mean that, in most countries, military views will be incorporated into national guidance sent from capitals to Permanent Representatives on the Security Council, rather than sent separately through MSC or other military channels.

Under the Chief of Staff, and in coordination, as appropriate, with civilian staff elements, the UN Military Staff would discharge a range of functions for the Secretary-General. These are needed for effective control of the military elements of peacekeeping and enforcement. At present, the Secretary-General lacks the professional military resources to carry them out. In brief outline, these staff functions would include:

- Providing military advice to the Secretary-General and the Security Council.

- Gathering and analyzing military information.

   Under article 99 of the Charter, the Secretary-General is charged with detecting and reporting threats to the peace, a task for which early and reliable information is essential. And planning and executing peacemaking and enforcement operations require a continuing flow of information. The UN Military Staff would be charged with military aspects of information analysis at headquarters, and of information gathering in the field, by means of observation, reconnaissance, liaison, and coordination with national sources of member nations. There would also be political input from other elements of the Secretariat as described in Chapter Three.

- Negotiating agreements for provision of national forces to the United Nations.

   Articles 43 and 45 of the Charter require agreements with member nations on the forces, facilities, and supporting arrangements each nation will keep available for the Security Council's call. Articles 48 and 49, calling for common action and mutual support by member nations may also require negotiation from time to time. The status of UN forces in various countries must be agreed. The UN Military Staff should provide military analysis for these agreements, and should advise and participate in negotiating with the contributing nations, which is a delicate political task requiring the leadership of the Secretary-General and his top deputies.*

• Preparing operating and coordinating directives for forces under UN control.

Forces that are assembled from several national establishments with differing organizational, operational and administrative systems, must be given two classes of directives to enable them to operate together. These are, first, UN general operations guidance, and, second, orders for specific operations.

The UN Military Staff should draft the operations guidance for the Secretary-General's approval, with extensive and continuing coordination with concerned civilian elements of the Secretariat and with representatives of member states that earmark forces. These guidelines should cover organizational structures, operational doctrines, communications, logistics, and administration. They should be distributed to member nations to permit them routinely to instruct and train their earmarked elements, and be regularly updated. The UN Military Staff should assist member nations in such orientation and training.

The orders for specific operations would include, for each instance, the basic operation plan and a series of orders covering its preparation, initiation, and execution within the mandate assigned to the mission.

• Command.

The Chief of Staff would be the Commander and the UN Military Staff would function as higher headquarters for the

---

* Such negotiations may require some adjustments in national-level organization, varying from country to country. In the U.S., they might be led by the State Department but would have to involve Defense and other agencies, suggesting a need for coordination by the National Security Council. Close Congressional liaison would also be required, even after general enabling legislation (as considered but not acted upon in 1946-47) was passed.

operational control of military forces assigned to the UN. The proposed UN Legion would have its own Force commander under the Chief of Staff. The Chief and Military Staff, which would exercise overall UN command for operational and administrative matters, would pass operational control for specific elements of UN forces to field commanders as necessary.

• Staff action for UN operations.

The UN Military Staff would perform normal military staff functions for the Secretary-General for each peacekeeping and enforcement operation, coordinating with civilian elements of the Secretariat. Tasks would include: determining the forces and support required; recommending who should be designated as field commander and determining his needs for staff and facilities; providing some personnel from the Military Staff to the field commander's staff to insure coordination; establishing effective communications with the field commander; issuing the necessary directives to the field commander for carrying out the operation as prescribed by the Secretary-General; arranging support, supply, and replacement or reinforcement to the operating forces; observing and reporting on the conduct of the operation and initiating or recommending necessary changes.

The United Nations Legion

UN forces, like those of virtually all historical alliances, are mixtures of national elements. They are made up, that is, of organized units drawn from national forces. These units, of whatever size, retain their national identity while serving the UN and carrying out UN assigned operations under UN assigned commanders. Their overriding loyalty must remain to their nations. Legally they continue to be governed by the laws and lawful directives of their nations; in case of conflict between UN and national orders, their legal requirement is to carry out the national orders. In jargon, they can be placed under the operational control of the UN, but they remain under the command of their national authorities. The national authorities consequently retain responsibilities for their units; they will properly insist on satisfying themselves about their proposed utilization and support before releasing them to the UN, and on their assigned tasks and support while so serving.

UN forces composed of national units are thus not instantly available to the organization, and not fully flexible operationally. These problems are, of course, in addition to the obvious difficulties of generating coordinated and mutually supporting action from elements with differing organization, training, doctrines, weapons, equipment, and, often, language. Also, national origins of organized units have political effect; they retain their national identities whether or not blue-helmeted, and their acts are inevitably seen as colored by their origin. In any given case, national hostility or fears of private national purposes can make one or several countries' forces unusable.

These problems confirm the utility of a military element that is not a unit of the military establishment of any country, a completely international standing UN Legion, under the Secretary-General and immediately available to the Security Council without requiring national concurrences for its deployment (assuming no veto is exercised in the Council.)   It could be dispatched rapidly wherever needed, even as a deterrent in anticipation of trouble, in what Secretary-General Boutros-Ghali calls "preventive diplomacy."[4] Constituent units could not be withdrawn by unilateral national action as has happened previously. It could be seen as a symbolic UN presence, a common UN Force, so integrated internationally that the national origins of the participants would be irrelevant. Potential adversaries, however, would also have to see it as the advance guard of the total military power available to the Security Council.

The size and composition of the UN Legion would necessarily be a compromise. It would have to be sufficiently large and capable enough to be of significant value in UN operations, combat and non-combat.   Only a working force that was able to carry out UN missions and, in fact, did so would justify creating it. The Legion could also be used in disaster relief situations when appropriate.   On the other hand, both financial and administrative economy would demand that its dimensions be kept modest.

A force on the following scale would meet these criteria during an initial formative and experimental phase: a single combined arms brigade task force with light infantry, light armor and high-tech mechanized elements, augmented by mobile artillery and helicopters, with engineer, signal and medical support. The headquarters and service units would be designed as the minimum necessary to permit independent administration, supply, maintenance and training. However, the force would have to be dependent on one or more national air forces for airlift and resupply and for combat air support. The total manpower of such a Legion would be in the 4,500 - 5,500 range.

If the initial force proves practicable and experience warrants, it should be expanded to three such brigade task forces, with limited air and naval support. That support might at first have to be provided by earmarked national forces (probably from the Quick Reaction Forces described below), but should as soon as feasible be integrated internationally and become organic to the Legion, in order that at least one of its brigades could deploy without the appearance of being tied to a member country's military establishment.

A brigade-sized force, rising to a division equivalent, would by itself be vulnerable to the superior forces of almost any mid-sized state; the Legion would of course be only a small element of the total military force available to the UN. However, even a small UN force, once organized and trained, would give the Security Council an asset which could be used for multiple purposes: establishing a quick UN presence, defending small nations, quickly reinforcing UN or national forces, manning a tripwire boundary, acting as peacekeepers or disaster relief teams, especially in hazardous places (as this is written Sarajevo is an example), carrying out special forces missions against terrorists or narcotics traffickers. Its members could be used for liaison, reconnaissance, observation, or as trainers, without need to call upon additional personnel from nations. Its purely international character would often make it more politically acceptable than national units.

The desirability of integration at the level of individuals may not be self-evident. Assuredly, creating such a force and bringing it to a state of military effectiveness, solving the political, ethnic, cultural, legal and language problems, would be a matter of great complexity. However, as discussed in Chapter Four, these problems are not insurmountable. Mixing national units -- and even elements of several services from one nation -- produces some of the same kinds of difficulties. Several experienced UN force commanders have said that efforts to join national platoons or companies into emergency defense forces have not been notably successful. They expressed the view that an integrated force of individual professionals who had trained together and had uniform equipment and doctrines would be more effective and have less cause for animosity. The integrated units could well feel that they were the vanguard of the future.

Eight NATO nations devoted several years of staff work during the 1960's to studying a proposed mixed-manned "Multilateral Force" (MLF) to provide a common nuclear deterrent force based on surface ships, and possibly with submarines, aircraft, and Pershing missile battalions. Although the plans for the MLF were shelved, and the Non-Proliferation Treaty precluded its creation, the conclusion of national experts, both military and civilian, was that such a commonly armed, jointly controlled and fully integrated force was legally, administratively, and operationally feasible.

In the UN Legion, the volunteers from national military forces would have to be seconded by their governments and accepted by the Legion. Ideally, they would be from elite units: paratroopers, marines, commando-rangers etc., known for their high morale and discipline. Individuals would need a high school diploma and fluency in two or more languages, one of them English. Tours of duty would be three to five years, with at least one reenlistment allowed by mutual agreement. The Legion would wear UN uniforms and be subject to a single disciplinary code. Its members would be paid by the Legion at a high common rate -- with the provision that a portion agreed between the home government and the UN could be banked for the individual or his family.

The UN Military Staff, perhaps after consultation with the Military Staff Committee, would determine the Legion's table of organization and equipment based upon recommendations from the initial commander and cadre. No single country or geographic region would be allowed more than a small percentage of the total manning, with NCO's and officers allocated proportionately. The Legion would have and own its regular equipment and armament; but since organic sea and airlift for the entire force would be prohibitively costly, the major part would be furnished (as is now the case for peacekeepers) under contract with governments or commercial carriers.

Despite the obvious problems, the political symbolism of a truly international UN intervention force would outweigh the difficulties and costs. The costs of a one-brigade start-up force, including the annualized portion of equipment, as well as operations and personnel are estimated to be in the range of $350 to $400 million per year. This assumes that new equipment would be selected from world-wide surplus stocks which could be obtained at less than cost. (The difficult problem of financing is addressed in Chapter Six below.)

It would be important to open the Legion to personnel from all UN members, not just those on the Security Council, in order to make it a truly symbolic global police force and to provide even small countries with at least a stake in the UN's new system.

The location and basing of the Legion would be only one of many problems. Ideally, it would be geographically dispersed, eventually with a brigade task force (and limited air and naval support) stationed at three strategically located bases. One might consider such sites as Cyprus, Canada or Panama, and the Philippines; many bases around the world are now becoming surplus during the post-Cold War retrenchments. Initially, one main training base would have to be selected, which could additionally serve the UN's existing and future earmarked peacekeeping and enforcement forces for UN training and exercises. Hopefully, one or more countries might offer to "host" the Legion during its experimental start-up phase.

Although very few of the millions of national military personnel around the world would have the opportunity to serve in the expanded Legion, military officers cite the value of the "Johnny Appleseed" factor, in which cadres of the Legion experienced in multinational planning and operations return to their national services. There they would serve as a nucleus for future UN actions in which their countries would participate and help to orient and train others. Desert Storm veterans point to the contribution which prior joint training and "cultural acclimatization" under NATO made to that operation's success.

The US program of military assistance and training has also provided "alumni" around the world capable of staffing international military operations. Some Eastern European countries are now included in such training; and at the April meeting of defense ministers of NATO and former Warsaw Pact countries, the suggestion was made for joint training and planning for peacekeeping operations. Such efforts could be valuable building blocks for the UN forces herein proposed.

National Forces for United Nations Duty

The vast majority of the military forces, facilities, and support needed for UN operations, peacekeeping and enforcement, must be obtained "on call," when a need develops, from the military forces and supporting structures of the member nations. The Charter drafters put the procedures for assembling enforcement forces in Chapter VII; they did not foresee the need for peacekeeping forces.

For enforcement, the Charter provides in Article 43 that individual treaties be negotiated by the Security Council with member countries (or groups of countries), to earmark the forces, assistance and facilities each would maintain at the Council's call and to specify their location and readiness.

The expectation was that major nations would earmark the bulk of their entire military establishments. The treaties were to be ratified by the signatory nations in accordance with their constitutional processes. The intent of the latter provision was to authorize the Security Council to call up the earmarked elements on its own authority, without need for further governmental approval by the providing nations, so as to avoid delay and dissension in the various national governments and make possible immediate coordinated action by UN forces.

It was expected that the forces called would be very large and powerful, on a WWII scale, and thus able to meet the sudden attack by a major aggressor that was then the overriding, almost exclusive, concern. Consequently all or nearly all the forces would come from the permanent members of the Council who had the major military establishments.

In brief, the Charter concept for enforcement forces was of pre-agreed, massive forces, largely from permanent members, immediately available on the Council's call. In practice, however, in the Cold War climate the permanent members promptly failed to agree on their earmarking, the Military Staff Committee personnel engaged in the attempt were withdrawn, and no attempt has ever been made to draft Article 43 treaties. The UN has no working machinery for enforcement forces.

Providing peacekeeping forces, on the other hand, has been accomplished through direct negotiations between the Secretary-General and the providing nations. Over the years, some nations and groups of nations --

notably the Nordic group -- have become steady suppliers and, especially for continuing operations, have usefully standardized their procedures. Generally speaking, however, each new mission starts from scratch and must improvise its methods.

Today, a need for enforcement action could cover a broad range of magnitudes and intensities, and arise nearly anywhere on the globe; the WW III scenario is far from the only possibility and, happily, it is the least likely. Peacekeeping calls increase in size and complexity; in some future operations it may be necessary to go beyond a position of pure neutrality and entirely peaceful action, blurring the boundary between peacekeeping and enforcement. It is time to produce a single, effective UN system, under the Charter, for calling up and controlling national contributions for all military operations of the UN.

The national elements for such a system logically fall into three categories: Quick Reaction Forces, Other Earmarked Forces, and Declared National Forces.

Quick Reaction Forces (QRF)

In a crisis, the major military powers represented on the Security Council at that time must be prepared to act decisively, on the basis of a prearranged system of "alerts" and extensive contingency planning conducted by the UN and national military staffs. Of the total national forces that countries are willing to "earmark" for possible UN service under Article 43 of the Charter, certain elements should be designated as "Quick Reaction Forces". Something analogous to a QRF is foreseen in Article 45. Each permanent Security Council member would be asked to assign a combat division (or the naval or air equivalent) and any country designated an alternating member or invited to join the Peace Management Committee would be asked to provide a ready combat brigade or the equivalent. Assigned units in QRF status could be rotated into and out of the assignment. For example, the U.S. might rotate an Airborne Division, a Marine Division, a naval carrier or amphibious task force, or an air wing to meet its QRF obligations. Taken together, several such divisions and brigades from a dozen or more countries could constitute an air mobile corps, with ample air and naval support, available on 48-72 hours notice, and the remaining divisions and brigades could provide a second, heavier, sea-transportable corps. These forces would, of course, be national in character, but when passed to the UN for a mission they would be under UN operational control and would respond to the UN chain of command. They would fly the UN flag as well as keep their own.

So that such forces would not be a mere aggregation, key elements would have to exercise together, with staffs trained in joint operations and in coordinating transport and logistic support.

Providing such Quick Reaction Forces, *at no cost* to the UN's already strained budget, might be regarded as an obligation stemming from permanent Security Council or near equivalent status. It would appear that these obligations could be met from forces in being without serious degradation of national force postures and readiness and without major additional cost. Some countries could best provide combat air support, lift, or amphibious capabilities, while others furnished primarily ground elements. UN Headquarters would select the best mix for the particular missions out of the total QRF available at a given time. To the extent possible, all would be elite volunteer national forces.

Contributions should be roughly equal among permanent members in terms of relative cost to the provider and of military equivalence. The same equality should apply among those who become alternating members or join the Peace Management Committee.[5] And countries would be expected to assign these forces to the UN at the Security Council's call in accordance with pledges made in advance, except only in case of "overriding" national emergency.

Other Earmarked Forces

All other forces earmarked for UN service would also be available for call, whether or not QRF elements had been previously called. They would, however, have a lower readiness status as negotiated in the treaties between the UN and the providing countries under Article 43. They would also have a lower presumption of automatic availability than QRF elements, and, unlike the QRF, the "earmarked" forces might have to be subject to greater UN reimbursement than the QRF. Peacekeeping forces, whose deployment is usually less time-urgent than for enforcement elements, would normally come from earmarked forces or from declared national forces.

The Article 43 obligation to "make available" forces to the Security Council applies to all United Nations members, not just those on the Council; all nations with usable military assets should earmark and should be ready to respond to the Council's call. The earmarking process should thus provide a detailed inventory of the military assets potentially available for UN deployment, including bases and facilities. At the time the call-ups were made, the forces to be called would have to be chosen and adjusted to fit the requirements of the specific operation. Close liaison would be needed between national authorities (and their UN representatives) and the Secretary-General and his UN Military Staff. The system, then, envisages an arrangement not unlike NATO's, albeit for a larger number of countries, to include periodic review of a country's forces, facilities, readiness, and adaptability to UN service.

Declared National Forces

These would consist of national military assets which countries were willing to "declare" to the UN so that they could be considered, and if necessary negotiated for, when a situation demanded, but which they were not willing to list among those earmarked for UN call. Some nuclear, special force, or paramilitary elements would presumably not even be declared. Such declaration to UN military authorities would provide the widest possible inventory of the military capabilities that the UN might call on, including the facilities and mutual assistance called for by Articles 43 and 49 for large-scale contingencies.

As a generalization, permanent members of the Security Council should be expected to declare a majority of their total forces and military resources, and to earmark perhaps half of those declared. Table III in Appendix B outlines the characteristics of the types of UN forces described above.

CHAPTER THREE

REFORMING UNITED NATIONS MACHINERY

Introduction

Since 1946, interested observers of the United Nations have urged that the Security Council be employed as a center for monitoring the state of the world and that it be encouraged to apply "preventive" or "quiet" diplomacy for the management of security and peace. Many look to the Secretary-General for leadership in this regard and point to his responsibility under Article 99 "to bring to the attention of the Security Council any matter which in his opinion may threaten the maintenance of international peace and security."[1]

Secretary-Generals have normally emphasized the use of quiet diplomacy in and outside the Security Council. In 1982, Secretary-General Perez de Cuellar began to lay the groundwork for creative diplomacy by the UN through routine, private and informal meetings of the Security Council, which by 1991 had been accepted in practice and proved to be successful.

In contrast to the use of quiet diplomacy, is the employment of the "Summit" with its accompanying political theater and compulsion for tangible accomplishments. The Charter provides for the Security Council to hold "periodic meetings at which each of its members may, if it so desires, be represented by a member of the government ..." In January, the Security Council, for the first time, met at the level of heads of government and gave an overarching directive to the United Nations and the Secretary-General in search of a desired new world order.[2]

In Chapter One the authors proposed ways to strengthen and make more representative the Security Council by adding five "Alternating Seats" which, they suggest, should rotate among ten to twelve major regional/global powers in a predetermined way. A Peace Management Committee, composed of those regional/global powers and the five permanent members, is also suggested. In this chapter we offer several proposals that we believe could improve the way the Security Council conducts its work. We suggest some tasks for the recommended Peace Management Committee, and offer additions as well as modifications to the responsibilities of a reactivated Military Staff Committee (MSC). With the delegation of some new functions to the MSC and the Security Council's assumption of duties originally expected of the MSC, there would be a necessary realignment of functions more in accord with current practices of democratic governments. Finally, the authors take up the need to strengthen the staff capabilities available to the UN Secretary-General and suggest a possible model for further staff restructuring in order to enable the Secretariat to carry out new and old tasks more effectively.

The Security Council

As an aid to achieving the UN's potential, the Security Council (and the Secretary-General) need a functional, high-tech Situation Center where, away from public scrutiny and the media, the authorized representatives and support personnel can together see and study real-time information, maps and displays about likely regional and global problems which are or could become challenges or threats to the peace. There they would be better able to anticipate and explore the opportunities for "quiet diplomacy," "good offices" or mediation; to determine whether to initiate an inquiry; or to take more pro-active peaceful settlement actions under Chapter VI or enforcement measures under Chapter VII of the UN Charter. There they should be assisted in following developments wherever the UN has a presence or interest. From there they should be able to communicate securely with governments and others, and to send to or receive from governments, UN Diplomatic Agents or UN Force Commanders, reports and instructions.

The Center might well be called "The Peace Room," as has been suggested by former Assistant Secretary-General Robert Muller and others. This proposed complex of information center and cabinet room might once have been described as a "War Room." Today, such a complex is vital for the maintenance of peace and the deterrence of war. The proposed UN facility would facilitate multilateral consideration of issues that could lead to peace or war, and promote common responsibility for the tasks and actions of the Security Council.

The Center should provide intimate consultation rooms and larger work and conference areas which would serve as a "crisis management center" when needed, and it could become a command center for overseeing any enforcement operations under Chapter VII of the Charter.

One useful model for such an international complex is at the seat of the North Atlantic Council in Brussels. The NATO Civil Staff and International Military Committee Staff maintain a secure conference and briefing room for reviewing situations of interest to the Council, particularly the deployment and activity of friendly and hostile forces. At any time, the 16 national representatives and the NATO Secretary-General can withdraw to an adjacent, private consultative chamber for confidential discussions among the principal representatives. Immediate and secure communication with NATO Major Commanders and member governments is at hand.[3]

It would be beneficial for the UN Security Council normally to meet once a week in private session for a briefing and discussion on international developments. Difficult decisions should be frankly discussed and, to the extent possible, resolved, at least provisionally, before the Council goes into public session. Thus, the monthly President of the Council, the Secretary-General or others would have an opportunity to attempt the resolution of issues before positions are hardened in public exchanges.

The Peace Management Committee

The Peace Management Committee, which the authors suggest should be established by the Security Council pursuant to Article 29, is intended to provide for the leading regional/global powers to join with the permanent members to support and advise the Security Council with respect to activities under Chapters VI and VII. The Committee should be composed of the Permanent, Alternating and other "contributing" UN members that are making available substantial "Quick Reaction Forces" and facilities for UN peacekeeping or UN enforcement measures.

The Peace Management Committee could assist the Council by

routinely providing regional and global assessments of possible challenges and threats to international order. Under the Committee's auspices, regional and functional working groups or "commissions" for the assessment of challenges to the peace might be convened periodically. Such groups, admittedly patterned after the North Atlantic Council's successful system, would be composed of senior policy planners and experienced diplomatic, military or intelligence officers.

Each group should be authorized to sponsor study groups of governmental and private experts on the subject under review. International nongovernmental organizations with the highest consultative status, as determined by the Economic and Social Council, should be accorded opportunities to present pertinent information. Following each session of a regional or functional commission or working group, a confidential report might be submitted to the Peace Management Committee, which in turn would report periodically to the Security Council.

Such systematic assessments should help to keep the Committee, the Secretariat (including the Military Staff) and the Council appraised of what may be required in the way of diplomacy, specific actions or preventive measures to keep the peace. The Secretary-General, his Military Staff and the Committee should regularly review the current and planned UN force structure, the holding of training exercises and other deterrent or "pacific measures."

Under the Security Council, the Peace Management Committee could also serve as the primary advisory group available to the Secretary-General for peacekeeping operations. A very important mission of the Committee or one of its subgroups would be to provide political guidance in the establishment and management of the UN Legion. In the spirit of Article 44, whenever significant forces of a UN member not on the Committee are participating in a military operation, that member should be invited "to participate in the decisions of the [Committee] concerning the employment of contingents of that member's armed forces."

The Military Staff Committee

The UN Military Staff Committee (MSC), composed of the Chiefs of Staff of the five permanent members of the Security Council or their personal representatives, is established by the Charter to advise and assist the Security Council. Today, however, the Security Council will want to reserve to itself (and thus to member governments) the political and political/military functions that the authors of the Charter imagined the MSC would perform. Examples of provisions which the Security Council may wish to subsume are Article 46 ("Plans for the application of armed force shall be made by the Security Council with the assistance of the Military Staff Committee."); Article 47, paragraph 3 (the MSC "shall be responsible under the Security Council for the strategic direction of any armed forces..."); and Article 47, paragraph 4 (the MSC "... may establish regional sub-committees."). The Security Council may decide to seek advice from the MSC in such matters on a case by case basis; but they will probably want primary counsel and support from the Secretariat, the multilateral Military Staff and from the Peace Management Committee.

There are several areas, however, not foreseen in the Charter where the assistance of the MSC could be valuable. First, the MSC with the support of their members' national military organizations -- and all five of the permanent members represented on the MSC maintain their own national intelligence systems -- should serve the Security Council and the entire UN as the designers and coordinators of a "United Nations Early Warning System," foremost against weapons of mass destruction, but also against any massive conventional military build-ups or attacks. Such information would be provided through the Council's crisis management center.

Second, such a UN Early Warning System could help the MSC serve the Security Council as the senior "Arms Control Supervisory Body," monitoring all arms control agreements registered with the UN or of concern to the security of its members. The MSC should promptly report observed infractions or terminations of such agreements to the Security Council.

Third, the MSC (with the support of the its members' national military organizations) could be requested by the Security Council to monitor the non-proliferation of weapons of mass destruction by providing support to the Secretariat, the International Atomic Energy Agency and other international organizations with responsibilities for such matters.

The Secretariat

The UN Charter establishes the Secretariat as one of the six "Principal Organs" of the United Nations, comprising the Secretary-General and his Staff. The Secretary-General (SG) is the "chief administrative officer of the Organization." He or his designee serves as the secretary of the General Assembly and its subsidiary bodies. Similarly, he serves the Security Council and its subordinate organs, except for the Military Staff Committee which has had its own staff. He has a similar role in the Economic and Social Council and its numerous bodies as well as in the Trusteeship Council. He performs such other functions as are entrusted to him by these entities.

The SG also serves as chairman of the Administrative Coordinating Committee which includes the chief administrative officers of the Specialized Agencies and coordinates their work. Not least, the SG annually makes a report to the General Assembly on the work of the organization, which can establish the themes for its annual session. It would be the understatement of the decade to say that the SG has a full plate of responsibilities.

The scope and responsibilities of the SG and hence of the UN Secretariat have grown for over four decades until it almost embraces the customary activities of a government. The present structure of the Secretariat reflects the periodic addition of responsibilities and offices, with some overlapping of jurisdiction. The present SG, Dr. Boutros Boutros-Ghali, has bravely begun some consolidations and rationalizations.* While the Secretariat is not and cannot be a government, some organizational steps in the direction of normal departments of government would make the whole more understandable to national delegations, governments and publics, upon whose support the United Nations and its Secretariat depends.

Happily, there is a logical division of functions long established in the work of the General Assembly, with its six-plus-one "Main Committees." They are: (1) Political, (2) Economic, (3) Social, (4) Non Self-Governing Territories, (5) Administration and Budget, (6) Legal, and as the seventh, Special Political, which generally deals with arms control, peacekeeping operations and security.

---

* However, after abolishing the former Secretariat Office of Research and the Collection of Information (ORCI), he may find that he must recreate and even augment it if he has to have the type of crisis management capability we think essential.

Consequently, it would seem logical to model a future Secretariat along parallel lines, as seven major departments and an Executive Office. The primary divisions might be as follows:

1. *Political Affairs,*
   to include General Assembly and Security Council responsibilities, along with the "Peace Room" or situation center, Future Challenges and Policy Planning, Regional Affairs (with Sections for the major regions), Pacific Settlement Matters, Mediation Services, and Representation and Protocol.

2. *Economic Affairs,*
   to include Economic Policy, Sustainable Development, Food and Agriculture, Transportation and Communication, Infrastructure, Finance, and Debts Management.

3. *Social Affairs,*
   to include Social Policy, Human Welfare, Education, Science, Culture, Humanitarian Activities, Housing and Habitats.

4. *Planetary Affairs,*
   to include the Environment, Natural Resources (Forests, Minerals, Oil and Water), Trusts and Non-Self Governing Territories, Oceans and Space and Geographic Survey.

5. *Administrative Affairs,*
   to include Program Analysis and
   Evaluation, Budget and Finance,
   International Organization,
   Personnel Policy, Conference
   Services, General Services, Internal
   Audit, Communications and
   Transportation.

6. *Legal Affairs,*
   to include Consular Questions,
   International Law, Human Rights,
   International Judiciary Affairs, and
   Civil Service Inspector General.

7. *Peacekeeping and Security Affairs,*
   to include Threat Assessment,
   Arms Control, Early Warning,
   "Peace Room" Technical Support,
   Crisis Management, Military Staff
   coordination, MSC Liaison,
   Peacekeeping Operations (Chapter
   VI½), Security Planning (Chapter
   VII agreements), Security Forces,
   Training and Operations, and
   Chapter VII enforcement.

8. *Executive Office of the Secretary-General,*
   to include SG's Private Office,
   Policy Management and Inter-
   departmental (and Inter-agency)
   Coordination, and Public Affairs.

The number of persons to whom such "ministerial" responsibility would
be delegated by the SG should, if possible, be limited to the eight. They
alone should be responsible for the above Departments, and should be

awarded the unique rank of "Deputy-Secretary-General." Each would then be authorized no more than one Under-Secretary-General and two Assistant-Secretary-Generals to assist them.

The UN Military Staff and Its Chief

The UN Military Staff and the UN Chief of Staff, which could logically be placed in the Department of Peacekeeping and Security Affairs, are the most important and needed innovations at the UN Headquarters for the reasons explained in the preceding chapter. There has long existed a Military Advisor to the Secretary-General and his office has gradually grown from one officer to five. They are overwhelmed by the responsibilities arising from the new world (dis)order and totally insufficient for the building of Chapter VII capabilities.

If the UN members are to enhance conditions for peace pursuant to the Charter, they will have to build a collective system for making, keeping and, enforcing peace. An effective system will have to include combined security forces under UN authority and sufficient immediate backup to make the system credible.

Therefore, the UN system must have a Military Staff and Chief under the SG and his Deputy for Peacekeeping and Security Affairs with the authorization to recruit, command, form, train, exercise and lead the national military made available by the UN members pursuant to the Charter. The Headquarters Military Staff is not intended to be a "Battle Staff," but a General Staff for strategic assessments and planning, forces preparation and coordination, to include logistic aspects, and political-military relations.

The UN Chief of Staff (that is, the senior military officer directly under the SG and his Deputy for Peacekeeping and Security Affairs) ought to have the rank of four-star General. He should have been the senior officer of a UN member's military service, been a successful field commander or otherwise have earned the respect of his peers. His appointment should come from the SG, after consultation with the MSC and the Security Council. He should serve at the pleasure of the SG, but normally for a term of three years with the possibility of one reappointment. The Vice Chief of Staff, a three-star, should be similarly qualified and appointed.

It is the suggestion of the authors that the UN Military Staff initially be structured along traditional military staff lines (1 through 6) with adaptation to the international and political-military character of the functions to be performed. Beginning with a practical limit of 200 officers, plus technical, enlisted, and civilian administrative personnel, the Military Staff could be distributed among seven Directorates and the Office of the Chief of Staff, namely: (1) Personnel, (2) Assessment, (3) Operations, (4) Logistics, (5) Plans and Policy, (6) Communications-Electronics, and (7) the Inspectorate General. Staffing guidelines should be provisional until experience leads to either their modification or confirmation.

The UN Military Staff should be drawn from all the Services. Because of the special nature of UN missions rough targets might be 40% Army, 25% Air Force, 20% Navy, 10% Marines or Special Forces, and 5% civilian specialists. Initially, each Directorate might be headed by a three-star General or Admiral and have one Brigadier or Major General as deputies. The immediate Office of the Chief of Staff might have two other General or Flag officers of one or two-star rank. The high number of such officers (18) is justified by their mission: to argue for men and resources; to coordinate efforts among international secretariats and governments; and to organize and lead forces composed of many different nationalities. Many of these officers may also be called upon to serve as Force Commanders or senior field staff for UN operations.

Each Directorate would need several functional divisions as well as regional specialists and would normally be headed by O-6s (Colonels or equivalent). Ideally, the regional experts within the functional Directorates should complement and reinforce each other and constitute a basis for political-military coordination with the Department of Political Affairs' own regional offices.

The listing below of the functional divisions under each Directorate is intended to provide an illustrative outline of what may be expected of the Military Staff and how its elements would complement one another. It suggests also that the staff of two hundred will be kept very busy. The organization set forth below indicates the approximate number of officers that may be needed. The higher headquarters requirements of the UN Legion are intended to be met within the Combined Military Staff and the Secretariat.

- C (for Combined) 1: Personnel Directorate (35 officers);
  Could include Divisions for Recruitment and Secondment, Units Acquisition; Enlisted and Officer Schools and Training; Performance, Promotion and Pay; Reserve, Separation and Veterans; Legal Affairs and Military Justice; and Regional Personnel.

- C2: Assessment Directorate (25);
  Could include Divisions for general Threat Assessment; Peace Management (e.g. situation room support); and Regional Assessment plus Technical Intelligence.

- C3: Operations Directorate (25);
  Could include Divisions for Force Capabilities, Force Training and Exercises; Peacekeeping Operations; QRF and Enforcement; and Regional Operations.

- C4: Logistics Directorate (35);
  Could include Divisions for Requirements; Equipment and Materiel; Supplies and POL; Transport and Facilities; Procurement; Finance; and Regional Logistics.

- C5: Plans and Policy Directorate (20);
  Could include Divisions for Futures Strategy; Plans and Doctrine; and Regional Strategy.

- C6: Communications-Electronics Directorate (35);
       Could include Divisions for Requirements; Inter-operability; Headquarters and Field Communications; Security; and Regional C-E Matters.

- C7: Inspector-General (25);
       Could cover such matters as readiness, ethics, complaints, and regional reviews.

The Office of the Chief of Staff would need some 20 officers over and above the 200 which have been listed on the Military Staff proper. They would handle coordination, protocol, and political-military matters (including coordination of Regional Divisions). They could also provide liaison with National Military Representatives, as well as providing staff support to the Chief.

In the view of the authors and those we have consulted, such a staff, reorganized as needed in light of experience, could handle the workload for the peace and security system we have proposed.

Regional Organizations

From the outset of drafting the UN Charter, regional arrangements and regional agencies were accorded a special place in the new global system. Chapter VIII, Article 52 makes clear that nothing in the Charter precludes them. Article 53, however, affirms that "... no enforcement action shall be taken under regional arrangements or by regional agencies without the authorization of the Security Council ... ." Nevertheless, Article 51 stipulates that nothing in the Charter "... shall impair the inherent right of individual or collective self-defense if an armed attack occurs against a member of the United Nations, until the Security Council has taken measures necessary to maintain international peace and security ... ." Thus, a permanent member of the Security Council could veto any Council decision which would override the implementation of this inherent right of collective self-defense.

It is important to recall that in the legislative history of Chapter VIII, it was conceded that the term "regional" was not limited by geographical proximity, but included the possibility of alliances and other collective arrangements that could be world wide.[4]

In the past several years, the usefulness of regional arrangements and agencies have become positive elements in the international security system. The European members of the UN, including the twelve which now comprise the European Community (EC), have been making use of the Western European Union (WEU) as its military agency. As such, it has functioned under the auspices of the United Nations in Desert Shield/Desert Storm and independently, but in coordination with the U.S., in other maritime protection operations in the Persian Gulf.

With respect to the current crisis in the former Yugoslavia, the Conference on Security and Cooperation in Europe (CSCE) has declared itself a regional organization pursuant to Chapter VIII of the Charter and has authorized both the North Atlantic Treaty Organization (NATO) and the WEU to take military measures on its behalf as well as on behalf of the United Nations. Therefore, the CSCE, NATO, and WEU could be said to be functioning as regional agencies under Chapter VIII. NATO has always viewed itself as a regional agency within the terms of that Chapter. In 1992, the North Atlantic Council extended the Alliance's possible area of concern and potential operations to the entire area of Europe, so that in the future it could become a vital arm of the UN Security Council for peacekeeping and enforcement.

Other areas of the world have seen similar developments in the use of regional arrangements and agencies. In Africa, the Organization of African Unity (OAU) has exercised with Chad the right of collective self defense against Libya. Peacekeeping measures and humanitarian intervention were undertaken under the OAU umbrella with respect to Liberia. In Latin America, the Organization of American States (OAS) has served both as a peacekeeping and enforcement agency with respect to the UN promoted settlements in Nicaragua and San Salvador.

The future is likely to produce more such collaboration. But it should be acknowledged that it may take many years before regional arrangements and agencies can become major building blocks of the World Security System.

For example, the Association of South East Asian Nations (ASEAN) has, as yet, no security functions at all. While we agree that the United Nations should use the auspices and local good offices of regional organizations when they are both available and likely to be effective, it must not allow itself to be hampered by their role in carrying out its own global mandates. For the Charter clearly indicates otherwise.

Unlike some other studies, we do not recommend any regional subcommands in the proposed UN security system. We do believe that small UN security liaison offices, probably attached to regional UN offices, could help to ensure that UN planning is geared to local realities and coordinated with planners in those regional organizations, such as NATO, which do have a security mission or potential.

CHAPTER FOUR

LESSONS FROM THE PAST

Introduction

Despite centuries of military coalitions, naval leagues and conglomerate armies, there are few precedents for the type and scale of United Nations forces we are suggesting. (Although Napoleon quipped that an enemy coalition was worth several divisions to his own side, the allies defeated him twice!) While there were multicultural elite guards such as the Ottoman Janissaries, most international forces were ad hoc, such as the embassy rescue forces put together during the 1905 Boxer rebellion in China. The UN's first Secretary-General requested the establishment of a multinational "UN Guard" of 5,000 men. But the Cold War environment permitted only the eventual creation of a civilian Field Service.

The UN's own 47 year history embraces 25 more or less consensual peacekeeping operations and two enforcement actions (Korea and Iraq) which were essentially international augmentation and ratification of missions undertaken by United States' armed forces. This chapter examines the lessons of that collective experience.

A particularly instructive model is the North Atlantic Treaty Organization (NATO) which has operated integrated commands and staffs, as well as specific operational elements such as the Allied Command Europe (ACE) Mobile Force, assorted Naval Standing Forces and the Airborne Warning and Control System (AWACS) with considerable success.

There can be little doubt that men from many nations and cultures can operate complex systems together; for much of the world's merchant shipping and civil aviation relies on multinational crews. One mandatory requirement, of course, is an ability to communicate in a common language; fortunately,

English is the international tongue of navigation, although Greek or Panamanian ships doubtless use the mother tongue for internal communication, even with foreign crews, with English as a back-up and for external purposes. A higher level of cooperation is required for international peacekeeping operations; but the experience of the UN has demonstrated that it can be attained.

On the other hand, the standards of cooperation and communication involved in the relatively peaceful task of peacekeeping are not as high as the levels of discipline, teamwork, and mutual confidence required in military combat. Although the French Foreign Legion is sometimes cited as an effective international fighting unit, it operates as an extension of the French Army, with French equipment, doctrine and training; it flies the French flag and is led primarily by French officers and NCOs. Although many ranks are filled by volunteers from other nationalities and races and the Legion has developed its own mystique and code of honor, it is not a truly "international" force. But two lessons from its experience are of interest.

Opinion polls show little or no political opposition in France to deployment of the Legion in far-off regions or on hazardous missions -- whereas similar deployments of regular French forces, especially conscripts, do arouse objections. The Foreign Legion is somehow thought to be "different" and it is composed entirely of volunteers.

A United Nations Legion, such as we have proposed, needs also to be different: an elite force of volunteers who supplement their national identity with a commitment to become military servants of the UN. And like the French Foreign Legion, the UN counterpart must undergo extensive and rigorous discipline and training, including simulated combat, to build the team work and mutual confidence needed if they do come under fire. This suggests that even recruits with established military skills will require at least a year of such training to become a fighting unit.

Some people hoped that the Franco-German joint brigade experiment might develop along integrated lines; but in the event, it became more of a military cultural exchange and language laboratory than an operational joint force. Although its members trained and studied together, the brigade maintained distinct French and German components, which seems likely also to be the pattern of the even more ambitious Franco-German corps announced in May 1992 to become operational as a "Eurocorps" in 1995.

Ironically, the most exhaustively studied approach to a truly common, integrated international military force never came into being. That was the proposed NATO Multilateral Force (MLF) for nuclear deterrence. The problems of such an unprecedented force and their prospective solutions were examined thoroughly by an eight-nation consortium in both civilian and military working groups over three years in the mid-1960's. We include the lessons from that proposal because its failure to come to fruition had nothing to do with any lack of operational feasibility.

The chapter concludes with some problems to consider and potential guidelines for drawing on all of the above experience if the United Nations decides to move ahead to establish its own Legion.

Part I: The United Nations Experience

The dispatch of small international coalitions of military observers, troops, election monitors, civilian administrators and police under United Nations auspices has come to be known as peacekeeping. As the organization adapted its available means to the maintenance of peace and security in a confrontational Cold War environment, peacekeeping became an innovation to carry out the collective security prescriptions of Chapters VI and VII of the Charter.

The history of peacekeeping operations[*] -- their compositions, commands, functions, and varying degree of success -- is characterized by ad hoc actions in response to particular security crises and the perceived interests of the UN powers that provided their mandate. During the Cold War, peacekeeping was essentially limited to conflict areas where both East and West perceived a common interest in stabilizing the situation. But even where there was such shared motivation, the success of peacekeeping operations was limited by many other factors. Often, the Security Council members differed over the extent to which a conflict should be resolved, the strength of UN deployment, and the degree and duration of involvement. Furthermore, the preservation of UN integrity and neutrality in peacekeeping and the consensual nature of its participation has always been considered vital by the Secretariat. This conservative approach limited the UN's capacity to meet the

---

[*] Table IV (Appendix B) provides a list of acronyms for UN peacekeeping operations.

challenges of far-reaching crises.

The result has been ad hoc initiatives by the Security Council, requests by local parties for mediation or peace-brokering, and a varied range of sizes, strength, composition, functions, mandates, and methods of financing for UN operations. We do not attempt to provide a comprehensive review of all UN peacekeeping for which other sources are available.[1] Rather we seek to distill a few lessons from the relevant experiences. Two things emerge from a thorough study of peacekeeping: First, conventional criticism of peacekeeping in terms of operational efficiency or success must be viewed in its historical context. In an effort to adapt to an environment that paralyzed its security arm, the United Nations extended the offices and resources of the Secretary-General and the international community the only way it could -- by reacting to each sensitive crisis in unique and realistic ways to prevent conflagration in the troublespots.

Second, UN peacekeeping has been a relative success despite its unsystematic approach compelled by, among other things, chronic lack of funds. The peace and security system outlined in this book does not therefore seek major reforms of the "blue helmet" function. It is vital to continue the type of conflict management that earned the organization's peacekeepers a Nobel Prize if it is to meet the challenges of the post-Cold War world.

Peacekeeping can be divided into two categories: operations limited to military observer missions, and those that include actual troops -- peacekeeping forces. We make this distinction because observer missions should remain unaffected by the changes required within the United Nations to enhance its peacekeeping capacity. Observer missions have been quite successful and their occasional failure has rarely resulted from logistical or structural constraints. In some cases, a mission was accomplished successfully but conflict returned because the underlying political conflict could not be resolved, as in Haiti.

Peacekeeping operations that included troops were almost by definition involved in more complicated situations where the United Nations felt that tensions required an armed capability, at least for defensive or deterrent purposes. We consider that more than 1,000 personnel constitute a "force," although the "observer" mission in Central American (ONUCA) involved 1,098 personnel. We have combined the dual operations in W. New Guinea (UNTEA/UNSF) and Cambodia (UNAMIC/UNTAC), which means the

United Nations has authorized 25 "peacekeeping" operations since 1948. Thirteen of these have occurred since 1987, showing the sharp increase in demand for such missions with the end of the Cold War.

If the UN is going to meet the challenge of increasing and expanding its operations, structural reforms will be needed within the Secretariat and especially in funding agreements dealt with in Chapter Six. Moreover, some of the past operations have suffered from a lack of political will by members of the Security Council while others lacked sufficient force to buttress their credibility.

We believe that our proposed system will make possible a greater number of effective peacekeeping operations that involve troops; that the relevant forces should be equipped to respond to a wider range of threats (assuming their support by the Security Coucil's five permanent members and regional powers); and that they must be allowed a greater, if still limited, strength to fulfill their mandate -- whether that is disarmament, demobilization, mine-clearing, armed protection of a local population, humanitarian aid, supporting a counter-insurgency, controlling fringe factions or enforcing a ceasefire.

This is not to de-emphasize the peaceful, political settlement of disputes. The distinction between peacekeeping and peace-enforcement must remain in principle. So must the prerequisite of local consent. But is it desirable to continue sending ad hoc, underequipped or untrained coalitions into potentially dangerous situations[2] when the international intent of the authorizing resolutions is to contain or resolve these conflicts? The brave men (and women) wearing the blue helmets deserve better!

Of the current 11 UN operations, five are over ten years old; two are over 40. If operations increase at the rate they have since 1988, the organization and its contributing members cannot afford failures or prolonged stalemates. Nor can the credibility of the UN itself afford that outcome.

Finally, many situations may emerge that require rapid deployments to establish a UN presence in a deterrent role. Depending on the crisis, a quickly activated UN Legion might be more suitable to fulfill such a mandate than the creation of an ad hoc peacekeeping coalition. That is for the Security Council to decide once the means become available.

The efforts that have gone into overcoming the complex coordination of ad hoc contributions; the delayed commitment of limited operational components; and the command and control problems of coalition forces with limited standardization of equipment and procedure have not been in vain. In fact, the UN managed to mount 25 such operations[3], 23 of them under separate financial budgets. That record argues that establishing a UN Legion and improving existing peacekeeping procedures requires primarily political and financial will and improved organization and advanced planning.

Peacekeeping Forces

The ten United Nations peacekeeping force operations* have had much in common. They have all involved in excess of 1,000 multinational troops deployed in response to civil or interstate conflict, often involving ethnic or religious strife. The actions in Cyprus, Syria, Lebanon, Cambodia and Yugoslavia are still in operation. Six of them have included support for an interim or restored governing body. Some have involved tasks as ambitious as conducting free and fair elections. Their size coupled with their unique composition and sensitive tasks really make these operations significant in the evolution of multinational cooperation.

Peacekeeping forces are naturally more effective in some roles than others. Verifying troop withdrawal, policing the separation of forces, monitoring borders, supervising elections and supporting democratic transition with the consent of local parties have been generally successful.[4] But they have not done that well in restoring governmental authority or detecting the illicit infiltration of troops or weapons.

As they evolve, UN operations are expanding to encompass broader responsibilities. For example, the force deployed to Croatia is expected to number almost 20,000 and supervise specific zones of conflict in the middle of a civil war, while that in Cambodia involves interim administration of

---

* This includes the dispatch of forces to Gaza in 1956 (UNEF I); the Congo in 1960 (ONUC); the operation to turn over West New Guinea in 1962 (UNSF); Cyprus in 1964 (UNFICYP); the second UNEF mission in 1973; the Syrian disengagement mission in 1974 (UNDOF); the existing force in Lebanon (UNIFIL); the transitional operation in Namibia in 1989 (UNTAG); and currently Cambodia (UNTAC) and Yugoslavia (UNPROFOR). Appendix A provides a comprehensive description of all ten peacekeeping forces discussed in this chapter listing data on location, strength, composition, costs, financing, objectives, preparation levels, fatalities etc.

government.

Experts who favor a less confrontational approach even in unstable international environments call for timely preventive measures to keep the peace.[5] Various studies conclude that the first six weeks is the critical period for establishing the credibility of a UN presence. In the past, however, peacekeeping forces were usually put together after conflicts had become deadlocked, when quick deployment was never feasible and often seemed undesirable.

This delayed reaction reflects a reality of peacekeeping during the Cold War (and again in the Yugoslavian crisis), and it leaves too much time for domestic or international tyrants to seize an advantage on the ground. The world would be better off if diplomacy and intervention were used to preempt conflict. Positioning peacekeepers on the Kuwait side of the Iraq border might or might not have deterred Saddam Hussein, but the rapid establishment of a UN presence in the future should help to deter states from violating international law, especially if that presence is an unquestionably neutral UN Legion. For the optimum preventive effect the standard response must be accomplished, not in six weeks, but in a matter of days. This turnaround will require reform, innovation and closer integration at the UN to create a more effective peace and security system.

Political Lessons

The original peacekeeping concept envisioned by Dag Hammarskjold should be reaffirmed. Any ambitious new plan must not undermine the credibility that these forces have earned under several guiding principles: authorization by the Security Council; use of force only in self-defense; impartial and neutral behavior in all circumstances; respect of state sovereignty; and local acceptance of the operations.[6]

If forces are deployed with the consent of only one party, UN peacekeepers should remain on the borders of the consenting party and be strong enough to pose at least the threat of escalation to involve a more substantial UN force. On occasion the Security Council has used its enforcement action power under Chapter VII of the Charter to pressure parties into accepting peacekeepers.[7] The most recent example was the observation mission deployed to Kuwait (UNIKOM) following its liberation.

The preamble of the mandating resolution indicates that the Council is acting under Chapter VII.[8]

But force commanders, acting alone, must not order their forces to initiate offensive operations, for that would seriously undermine the UN role as an instrument of peace. The escalation from peacekeeping to enforcement must come from a Security Council mandate after it determines that a legitimate violation of international law has occurred. While commanders of purely national forces often have the power to react to changes in their situations, only the Security Council can make such a decision for UN operations. This reality supports the need, discussed in earlier chapters, for situation reporting, military assessment capabilities and rapid implementation of Council decisions by an effective UN military staff.

The history of UN peacekeeping also suggests that situations ripe for force deployment rarely develop until parties to a conflict see a political, economic or military risk to their national interest in continuing hostility. Furthermore, deployment has usually occurred after prolonged conflict produced a stalemate or when the big powers shared an interest in interfering. The first and second force deployments in the Suez in 1956 (UNEF), in the Sinai in 1973 (UNEF II), and in Lebanon in 1978 (UNIFIL) were the result of Security Council initiatives. The decisions to help disengage forces after the 1973 October War (UNDOF) and construct Namibia in 1989 (UNTAG) were both made in conjunction with U.S. mediation. In Cyprus (UNFICYP), it was the United Kingdom that requested peacekeepers; and both Cambodia and Yugoslavia are the result of initiatives and support of most, if not all, the five permanent members.

It follows that active support of the big powers, especially the United States, is a requirement for the success of future operations. The end of the Gulf War marked another milestone for the Security Council when all five permanent members contributed to the postwar observer mission in Kuwait (UNIKOM). We believe the Security Council should use this symbolic representation in future operations that include peacekeeping forces. Physical presence of the five permanent members even in small numbers in these operations would substantially enhance political credibility for collective security, although a majority of forces might continue to come from small, medium and regional powers.

The disappearance of the East-West confrontation raises the question of what interest will motivate the West to get involved in conflicts in the developing world. Will its reluctance to cope with Yugoslavia be a model for the post-Cold War era? It is critical to the future of the United Nations that the large powers demonstrate their willingness to promote international peace and security by using the veto with great restraint and adding resources and political symbolism to an expanding peacekeeping agenda. They must also demonstrate the quality of persistence and of staying power, even in difficult cases involving casualties.

Technical Aspects of Peacekeeping

Studies on how to improve the effectiveness of peacekeeping are becoming quite prevalent in academic and government circles.[9] While many deal solely with the political, legal or financial aspects, some treat more technical questions. It is crucial that we tackle the hard issues such as staging, logistics, communications, and intelligence. These are some of the problem areas:

• Procurement perhaps from military surplus or other national stocks, of the necessary equipment and supplies;

• Gathering of information prior to troop deployment (including location of mine fields, condition of local transport, and disposition of local forces); Access to vital "real-time" intelligence from satellite and other sources;

• Compilation of mission planning data and tactical surveys (upgrading the Office for Research and the Collection of Information);

• Development of a standard operating procedure (expanding on the Nordic model);

• Maintenance of dispersed and expanded storage facilities;

• Division of command between UN military and civilian

officers and the communication and support of Headquarters in
New York; Use of UN field offices for additional support;

• Acquisition of permanent training and staging bases for
quicker deployment of peacekeeping forces;

• Use of sophisticated military technology to accomplish
surveillance tasks vital to the success of many missions;

• Notification of local parties of UN movements to build
confidence and prevent unnecessary conflict; rules of
engagement should also be improved;

• Training of civilian, police, or military personnel in language
and other skills to enhance their potential for UN assignment;

• Provisions for quicker air- and sea-lift capacity for UN troop
deployment at reduced rates or for paying off arrears by
providing lift services "in kind."

An elementary step toward operational improvement is for member
states to quickly complete the peacekeeping resource questionnaires that the
Secretary-General circulated in May 1990 and again in 1992.[10] The fact that
only a handful of countries have replied to these suggests a low national
priority for supporting the organization's work and reveals a lack of sufficient
contact between the UN and many military establishments.

Only when the SG and his staff have an adequate estimation of what
has been pledged can contingency planning begin. Other studies have pointed
out that peacekeepers often lack the basic vehicles needed on a mission.
Jeeps and personnel carriers can only be ordered from commercial
manufacturers after a mission has been approved. This can involve months
of delay and undermine quick deployment. A stock of vehicles and
equipment must be maintained.

Under-Secretary-General for Peacekeeping Operations Marrack
Goulding and the Special Committee on Peacekeeping continue to stress the
seriousness of these problems. The $2.7 billion cost of current operations is

two and a half times the regular UN budget. This is relatively small compared to the costs of failure, but states continue to define their own schedules of payment, undermining the very operations they have authorized.

It will not be easy to implement the above recommendations, but the task can only begin with the functioning of a structure in the Secretariat as designed in Chapter Three. The key military powers on the Security Council could quickly provide substantive improvements in the quality of peacekeeping. The sensitive area of intelligence and technology sharing has engendered little agreement within the UN. But contributions of reasonably sophisticated weapon and surveillance technologies would dramatically improve peacekeeping without endangering national security. The missions of "blue helmet" peacekeeping and the UN Legion should never come into conflict with the advanced technologies of countries like Russia, Germany or Japan.

One approach is the deployment of special national detachments to peacekeeping forces. A U.S. detachment that could operate and maintain ground radar, night vision devices or even something as large as a Patriot missile system, could theoretically do so without giving away military technology. This type of compartmentalized support by nationals of one country would eliminate the need to train nationals of other countries in sensitive technologies and might guarantee the success of an operation.

While this is not the place to debate the issue, proposals for a UN intelligence satellite that have been put forward now merit serious consideration. As UN operations increase, it is critical that any Peace Room facility have access to real-time information to assess the security of a mission and inform the Security Council. While all of this information is available to the defense departments of the permanent members, the Secretary-General and his staff are uniquely qualified to analyze and inform the Council objectively so it can make decisions. Finally, remote sensing verification is one area where the UN can greatly improve its effectiveness, and thoughtful proposals to that end deserve more attention.[11]

Mandates

If the world decides to turn consistently to the United Nations to respond to threats to peace, it becomes more crucial than ever for the

Security Council to state clearly an operation's purpose.[12]

While vital roles are being filled by long-standing missions -- in the Middle East (UNTSO, UNIFIL, and UNDOF), Cyprus (UNFICYP), and India/Pakistan (UNMOGIP) -- their annual cost and longevity pose the question: How far can the United Nations go? With existing finances, the answer is not very far. But two views are emerging. One side maintains that the UN is uniquely qualified to maintain a permanent presence in the persistent trouble spots like Cyprus. Governments, citing financial limitations, may argue for a limit to the UN's span of activities, especially while it undertakes more ambitious projects. Such limits or "sunset provisions" may reassure those who are skeptical about increasing their UN contributions.

But even with an expanded and improved Secretariat, the organization cannot afford to support missions that will fail because their mandate is politically weak or operationally unfeasible.[13] Furthermore, as the UN develops different levels of response, it must use its instruments more carefully than ever.   Confronted with the possibility of upgrading a peacekeeping operation to an enforcement action, it must precisely examine the shortcomings: Is the force too small? Is the mandate too weak?

In Lebanon, UNIFIL has served many functions with clearly limited success.   Study suggests that force is not the solution.   Expanding its deployment zone, granting it power to disarm combatants, containing retaliation and continuing to press the parties into negotiation would likely be more successful.[14]

In some situations, a conflict may simply not be ripe for solution, and no amount of further action is going to convince parties that settling for less than total victory is not a defeat. Cyprus comes to mind, as well as the crisis in the Congo.

In the Congo, virtual anarchy resulted from a mix of political turmoil, fundamental conflicts of superpower objectives, and a United Nations struggling to define a peacekeeping role in a situation that involved domestic intervention. It is foolish to second-guess Hammarskjold or the ONUC Force Commanders but according to Sir Brian Urquhart, the decision to involve peacekeepers in offensive combat in September 1961 was a grave one.[15]

This example illuminates the necessity of preserving the political integrity of peacekeepers. But the difficult problem of "transitioning" from peacemaking to peace-enforcement has never really been faced, except that peacekeepers in the Congo were forced to assume a de facto enforcement role in the face of Soviet hostility in the Security Council (at a time when Soviet policy was to support all "wars of national liberation"). Historically, peacekeeping was an extension of the Chapter VI peaceful settlement provisions; enforcement was strictly a Chapter VII concept used only in Korea and Iraq. "Never the twain shall meet" was the unspoken attitude of many at the UN, since the essence of peacemaking was the non-use of force except in self-defense and required the basic neutrality of the blue-helmeted "Soldiers Without Enemies" as one study called them.[16]

Now, however, the SG's report "An Agenda for Peace" has recognized the continuum of activity from prevention to peacemaking to peacekeeping to enforcement, and Yugoslavia has dramatized how several functions can be needed concurrently, such as peacekeeping, humanitarian relief and armed protection.

We think it important that peacekeeping be kept neutral at the political levels, insofar as possible. Operationally, however this is more difficult. How should peacekeepers respond to sustained attack? Don *olive-drab* helmets and pick up their rifles? Withdraw? Surrender? Even if heavier weapons (tanks and artillery) were airlifted in for defensive purposes would the personnel be trained to use them?

Combat-trained units can be cross-trained in peacekeeping roles; but the reverse is not necessarily true. For the average infantry rifleman cannot always handle sophisticated crew-served weapons. Does the UN then have to withdraw its Chapter VI½ forces while Chapter VII (or VII½) units are brought in? And can the UN system afford two types of units? We believe that some situations can be judged "safe" for peacekeepers only. But others -- Cambodia, Yugoslavia, and Iraq may require both peacekeeping and combat capabilities. In this type of case, and in the emerging new category of what Secretary-General Boutros-Ghali calls "armed protection" (such as the anarchy, famine and humanitarian disaster in Somalia) cross-trained units such as the proposed Legion should be used in danger spots with concurrent alert of the Quick Reaction Forces to deter escalation or deal with escalation by the hostile party.

We believe that enforcement should only become an option available to the United Nations within a comprehensive peace and security system.[17] When the Security Council decides that a peacekeeping force is failing to accomplish clearly stated tasks it should re-define the goals of an operation. In order to safeguard the lives of its peacekeepers (or Legionnaires) or respond to an increased threat, the UN needs the proper machinery to assess and react promptly to new situations, such as by alert and precautionary deployment of Quick Reaction elements.

Furthermore, to enhance its peacekeeping capacity, the UN will have to use all of the instruments at its disposal. Any restructuring must not de-emphasize the tools it has used in the past. If the United Nations is to identify potential troublespots, exercise preventive diplomacy, deploy early deterrent force (or maintain a cease-fire), pursue political settlement and most importantly, create peacekeeping forces with a clear mission; it must have an integrated system that can fully implement its resolutions.

Past Enforcement Operations

The foregoing discussion has been limited to peacekeeping operations. As noted elsewhere, the UN's only experience with Chapter VII enforcement has been in Korea and in Desert Shield/Storm. Both were primarily U.S. military operations with UN approval and the participation of selected allies. Korea did have a UN "Command" -- which still functions, in name at least, through double-hatting of the U.S. field commanders. For the most part, the U.S. also supplied the logistic support for the allied contingents and in a few cases helped to pay for them through military assistance and other programs.

Desert Shield/Storm did not even involve a formal UN Command. Rather, a U.S. Command worked with independent allied commands for various Arab nations, especially Saudi Arabia, as the host country for the force buildup, and with the European allies constituted an ad hoc coalition under the overall "theater" command of U.S. General Schwarzkopf. There were, however, consolidated Air Operations Centers for coordination and generally good liaison between headquarters, although there were serious shortcomings in intelligence and problems with communications. Of the total costs of $61 billion, the allies (including Germany and Japan which did not send troops) contributed nearly $54 billion. Although U.S. officers have called the coalition operation "a political dream and a military nightmare," it did work with astonishing operational success on the battlefield.

Given the right political environment, the Korean and Gulf war models would be one of the most cost-effective ways to proceed for other operations, since a single country (the U.S.) would provide a common command and logistic structure with large ground, air and sea combat elements while others contributed smaller forces or financial support, or both. However, it is the thesis of this book that such models will not be acceptable in the future to either U.S. or world opinion, so that the UN itself must develop the military capability to act in its own name and that of all its members.

Part II: Other Multinational Lessons

The Franco-German Experiment

Primarily at France's initiative, in 1987 the French and German governments formed a joint Council On Defense and Security with, inter alia, the mission of supervising a Franco-German Joint Brigade. It had been announced in 1984, but no troops were actually assigned to the unit until 1987. Based near Stuttgart, Germany, it consisted of a Headquarters and Headquarters Battalion with supply services, a French battalion, and three German companies -- housed in separate barracks. The 4,000 man brigade was commanded by a French general with a German colonel as Deputy Commander. Operational control was to be decided by the two governments.[1]

The Germans were from territorial units, i.e. those not assigned to NATO, while the French troops were primarily from the Alsace region, giving them some familiarity with the German language. The Germans were usually one year conscripts with little knowledge of French.

The brigade's operational mission was primarily rear area security. Only the headquarters was mixed, drawing on bilingual personnel; the operational units remained national in identity, uniforms, and in their legal, administrative and pay systems. Even the equipment was national, so that some of it, assault rifles for example, was not "interoperable" -- a long-time NATO goal. While the brigade therefore did not fulfill initial hopes that it might become a laboratory for mixed forces, it may have served as a political symbol, a cultural acclimatization experience and a language school.

Language remained a significant barrier, and cultural differences persisted. Germany provided the housekeeping and common mess arrangements, leading to frequent culinary complaints from the French -- who formed their own canteen, also open to German personnel, provided they paid in French currency. (Similarly, American Post Exchanges in Europe are open to allied personnel, but payment must be in dollars.)

The decision in May 1992 to expand the brigade into an army corps with a planned strength of 35,000 was more of a political decision, again initiated mainly by France, than the normal expansion of a successful experiment.[2] It will reportedly have two German mechanized brigades and a French armored division, still separately commanded and supported, but administered by a joint headquarters with alternating levels of French and German command. Its eventual mission -- the corps is not expected to be operational until 1995, may evolve simply as territorial or rear area defense; or it may be assigned to another French corps or to a NATO corps. In apparent preparation for such enlargement, the existing brigade is being moved from a single caserne to several other locations near Stuttgart.

There has also been talk of making the new corps available for peacekeeping-type missions outside the NATO area, which would pose a problem for the Germans until they have passed enabling modifications to existing constitutional restrictions.

Other members of the European Community and the Western European Union have been invited to participate in this "Eurocorps," but only hints of future interest, rather than implied force commitments have been received so far. The United States and Britain have responded coolly to this development, voicing suspicions that it may undermine NATO commitments.[3] The French, and to a lesser extent the Germans, see it as the seed corn of a "European" defense capability once the day comes, as many French believe it will, that U.S. forces leave the continent. They also view it as another avenue for building a more unified Europe.

In short, the future is open. It is too soon to forecast the direction in which this or other developments in European security mechanisms may evolve. But two lessons for the United Nations forces, or at least the Legion, can be drawn from the Franco-German experiment to date: first, the importance (and difficulties) of fluency in a common language and the persistence of cultural differences, especially in regard to food; and second, that to be truly international, a force must be mixed-manned, that is, integrated at lower operating levels, rather than just at headquarters, and have common equipment and doctrine.

NATO's Experience

The North Atlantic Treaty makes no provision for any "organization" beyond a Council and a Defense Committee to implement the provision that "an armed attack against one or more..(parties)...shall be considered an attack against them all." The organization developed ad hoc in response to external events such as the Korean War and perceived Soviet threats in Europe. Allied Command Europe and its Supreme Headquarters (SHAPE) only became operational in Paris in April 1951, a full two years after the treaty was signed in Washington. But over the next four decades a major alliance system was forged, embodying an elaborate civilian and military staff structure, and numerous intergovernmental bodies, ranging from the North Atlantic Council and its committees to various production and logistics agencies.

On the military side, NATO has two major international commands (SACEUR and SACLANT, for Europe and the Atlantic) and has had a Channel Command. It is to be subsumed into Allied Forces Northwest in the reorganization planned for 1993. The North American Air Defense Command (NORAD) is a bilateral U.S. and Canadian effort.

Space precludes any detailed account of the history of NATO's structural evolution but ample material is available elsewhere.[4] The most applicable experience from the United Nations perspective is that of SHAPE, the International Military Staff and the combined operating elements such as the ACE Mobile Force, the Standing Naval Forces and the airborne warning (AWACS Forces) command. The NATO common infrastructure program is also of interest.

It should be stressed that although NATO's headquarters functions are internationally integrated, the combat elements are built on purely national force elements, with their own national logistic support, and integrated only at the level of army or corps commands, that is to say, national divisions (or corps) combined into a larger international force. (In general, alliance forces are either "assigned" to one of the NATO commands, as is the case for most German armed forces, or "earmarked" for assignment and the passage of actual command at a later date, such as U.S. divisions which would be moved to Europe in a crisis.)

As NATO shifts from a linear "forward" defense concept with national zones of responsibility to more mobile multinational corps, this pattern seems likely to continue, posing new problems of logistic support and -- notwithstanding decades of effort to promote standardization and "interoperability" of equipment -- of compatibility.

The U.S. insisted from the beginning that "logistics are a national responsibility," fearing that otherwise it might have to supply all the allied forces. Such early standardization as had been produced by U.S. military assistance programs was overtaken by obsolescence and pressure from national armaments industries for their government's support of particular weapons systems. Although many co-production schemes were developed, involving consortia of two or more NATO countries, and there has been some progress in standardization, many observers count the failure to integrate and rationalize NATO's defense production systems as the Alliance's major shortcoming. Denying the economies of centralized procurement and of scale has probably added as much as 35% to NATO's combined defense costs. However, this lesson can not be applied to a United Nations military effort. For what proved politically impossible for a solid alliance of 16 nations would surely prove unobtainable for a looser grouping of ten times that number.

Another of NATO's lessons, however, is applicable. This is the concept, nowhere written as such but implicit in the treaty,[5] that "any number can fight." In other words, an attack on one of NATO's flanks could be met by the regional countries plus say, forces from Britain, France and the U.S. without having to wait for all members to respond or even concur. There is thus no veto applicable to NATO, although the Council generally operates by consensus and it would be difficult to carry out some military actions without nearly full alliance concurrence and participation.[6]

At the United Nations, this should mean that the permanent members of the Council will exercise their veto only in matters of supreme national interest and abstain, as China did on Iraq, when a majority feels it necessary to authorize military action. No one was obliged to participate in the Gulf operations; but those who felt it important to do so were free to act.

From the very beginning, NATO's supreme headquarters under General Eisenhower carried forward the principles of international staffing and command which he had developed as leader of the World War II European campaigns. Because of the key role played by U.S. forces, and particularly their nuclear capabilities, many commands are two-hatted, with SACEUR also being the U.S. Commander in Chief, Europe (CINCEUR).

As a primarily naval organization headquartered in Norfolk, Virginia, SACLANT's organization is somewhat different from that of Allied Command Europe (ACE) since its operating responsibilities are more dispersed over the vast sea and littoral areas through which lines of supply and communications must be secured from North America to Europe; but the principle of international staff and command is maintained as much as possible.

Organized with primary attention to land and air defense, Allied Command Europe (ACE) has had (thus far) an American SACEUR with two Deputies of other nationalities, one of whom coordinates nuclear planning. The Command has been divided regionally into Northern, Central, and Southern European subcommands, and further into commands for specific areas and functions, e.g. land forces, air forces, and in the case of the Baltic and Mediterranean, naval forces. In 1993, there will be one primary command, AFCENT with major land and air components.

At both headquarters and senior command levels, the staffs are international although nationally paid, drawing particularly on officers from countries in the region concerned, who have developed effective teamwork in years of training and regular exercises, both in the field (or at sea) and through CPX (Command Post) Exercises which often are now computer-assisted war games. While no one can divine what would have happened in the "fog of war" -- especially a nuclear conflict, most observers credit NATO with the ability to carry out its missions, sufficient at least to maintain a credible deterrent to aggression for forty years. Liaison with member governments occurs at many levels, supported on the military side by the presence of National Military Representatives at SHAPE Headquarters. A similar function would have to be carried out in any enhanced United Nations system.

NATO's Military Committee (the Chiefs of Staff of the members) is the highest military authority in the Alliance to which the major commands report. It is subordinate to the North Atlantic Council. Its members generally elect their Chairman for a three year term, while the essentially honorary Presidency of the Committee rotates annually. The Chairman is supported by a Director of the International Military Staff (IMS), comprising some 150 officers, 150 enlisted men, and 100 civilians.

The Military Committee and its staff are now co-located with the Council and the civilian International Staff at NATO headquarters in Brussels. Under the Director of the NATO International Military Staff are such services as a Secretariat, Public Information Office and Comptroller. The Staff itself is broken down into six major divisions, each with two or more branches. The divisions are responsible for: Intelligence, Plans and Policy, Operations, Logistics and Resources, Communications and Armaments and Standardization. This staff could serve, with adjustments, as one possible model for the United Nations Military Staff discussed in previous Chapters.* As explained there, we do not think the NATO Military Committee model, as reflected in the UN's Military Staff Committee, can be adapted to the enhanced UN system we are recommending, although the MSC can serve as an advisory and coordinating body.

Originally, the NATO Military Committee was spearheaded by a Standing Group, or executive committee of Britain, France and the U.S., which was located in Washington. With the withdrawal of France and the move of NATO to Brussels, the Standing Group was abolished in 1967 and the IMS was created on an enlarged basis in Brussels.

The geographic and cultural separation between NATO's military and civilian staffs, along with the predominant role of SACEUR, led to problems of political-military coordination and revealed a need for greater integration of strategy, forces and budgets. In NATO's earlier years, the strategy of massive (nuclear) retaliation bore little relationship to the force structure of the alliance (too big for a tripwire and too small for conventional defense) or to the national defense budgets which were supposed to support the forces. During the Kennedy Administration and with the leadership of American Defense Secretary McNamara and British Defense Minister Healey, this began to change.[7]

In 1967, the nuclear response emphasis of MC 14/1 was replaced after years of debate within the Alliance by the so-called flexible response strategy embodied in MC 14/2. That, in fact, was mandated by the guidance of the Defense Ministers in the Defense Planning Committee of the Council. Planning procedures were also revised to blend military, political and

---

* The relatively small size of the IMS was decided with a view to the nearby availability of additional staff resources at SHAPE. A UN Military Staff, lacking that resource, might have to be somewhat larger.

economic factors instead of relying on purely military "requirements" (which were in many instances quite unrealistic); and a rolling five-year planning cycle was adopted.

These changes improved the political-military relationship and led to a more effective partnership between the Council, the Military Committee, SHAPE, the IMS and the international civilian staff. This paralleled and in some cases may have aided the development of civilian control and coordination in national capitals.

There are important lessons here for the development of the United Nations peace and security system:

• Political considerations will always be dominant (even more so at the UN than with NATO) so the UN Chief of Staff and his military staff must be clearly subordinate to the Security Council and work closely with the elements of the Secretariat responsible for peacekeeping and enforcement.

• Military planners must be oriented from the beginning to work with forces likely to be available, based on the Article 43 and other agreements to be negotiated, and not on what they would like to have, i.e. on "purely military requirements."

• As a corollary, the civilians dealing with the political aspects of UN operations must give appropriate weight to professional military judgments about what a given force can, and cannot, be expected to accomplish.

• Effective national military representation is a vital part of national missions to the UN and they must have close ties to defense establishments in capitals.

• Personnel selection and assignments are critical to the effectiveness of international military (and civilian) staffs. Loyalties while serving must be to the United Nations itself, rather than to national governments or services. A suggestion on this is made below.

All of this will not be easy in a global community where many members' military establishments are part of the national political power structure, or where (as in most communist or former communist countries) "civilian control" -- as contrasted to party and secret police control -- is rudimentary at best. (This is one of the reasons for not upgrading the role of the long-dormant MSC and developing instead an integrated military staff at UN headquarters.)

Because the UN has some 175 member nations, in sharp contrast to NATO's sixteen, a "quota" system for selecting staff will not do. Obviously, however, some balance must be maintained among regions. We believe that there are now enough military alumni who have served in UN capacities to warrant establishing a nominating board composed of senior retired officers. They would propose slates of officers with international track records (counting NATO and other alliance experience) for UN military service at both command and staff levels. Countries would be invited, but not obligated, to second these individuals.

We believe that the resulting pool of officers would be among the best available for UN duty and would avoid the practice of politically rewarding certain officers (or getting them out of the way) by giving them a UN billet. Indeed, the UN may increasingly become where the "action" is instead of a military backwater. One of the requirements for promoting U.S. officers to general or flag rank is service in international capacities and in integrated organizations, such as the Office of the Secretary of Defense. A similar criterion in other nations would enhance the career desirability of UN service.

INFRASTRUCTURE

Since its inception, NATO has operated a common infrastructure program for the construction of bases, airfields, telecommunications (including satellites), war headquarters, ports, pipelines and storage facilities. Also included were the ground environment, e.g. radar systems, etc., for NATO's integrated air defense (NADGE) program. NATO has also developed coordinated, and to some degree common, command, control, consultation, information and data processing systems and organizations.

Up through Infrastructure Slice 41 (1990), over 6 billion "Infrastructure

Accounting Units" -- analogous in purpose to the European Currency Unit (ECU) but now worth about 3½ U.S. dollars per unit -- or some $US 20 billion were spent by the alliance.

The infrastructure cost-sharing formula is adjusted by the North Atlantic Council from time to time, but the U.S. share was reduced over the years from 47% to 24%, with Germany now paying over 25%. The details of the program, its planning, financing, auditing and inspection, and international competitive bidding procedures are too complex for discussion here.[8] But the rationale is that facilities in a given country which are for the use of common or allied forces should therefore be managed and financed in common.[9]

If the UN Legion is established at several bases, as would be desirable, with common training facilities or elements of the Quick Reaction Forces and headquarters detachments, a similar principle would undoubtedly have to apply -- as it already does to the costs of UN Headquarters in New York and elsewhere.

There are hundreds of military bases around the world now becoming surplus under the post-Cold War build-down, and some prospective host countries might offer them free of "rent" in exchange for the economic value of the UN presence. But most would require substantial additional construction for troop housing (and for accompanying families, if that was deemed essential to morale) and other Legion facilities, such as communications. Initially, perhaps, during the inaugural-experimental phase, this could be held to a minimum for a brigade-sized force.

However, a Legion of three or four times this size with some indigenous tactical air and limited naval support at three or more bases around the world would be a much more expensive proposition. It probably could not be handled through the UN's present headquarters budget. It could, however, be much smaller and less complex than NATO's infrastructure program, which had to prepare for combat operations and war headquarters as well as peacetime facilities. It could probably be handled at the political level by the Peace Management Committee of the Security Council which we have proposed, serving as a type of executive committee for oversight and negotiation of cost-sharing, much as the North Atlantic Council does for NATO.

OTHER NATO FORCES

As noted earlier most "assigned" NATO forces remain under national command in peacetime and only pass to NATO control at specific phases of the alert system. More interesting, from the standpoint of an enhanced United Nations system, are the exceptions.

These include air defense units on alert (now stood down) including airborne early warning (AWACS), the ACE Mobile Force (AMF) and Standing Naval Forces. While the UN would not need its own AWACS, parallels for a UN satellite system for communications or even verification purposes might develop in the future, so that infrastructure principles might apply.

The AMF, in the measured words of the NATO "manual"[10] is: "a small, multinational task force which could be sent at short notice to any threatened part of Allied Command Europe to demonstrate the solidarity of the Alliance and its ability and determination to defend itself against aggression." In other words, an aggressor would find himself shooting at all sixteen flags of the alliance, not just one or two -- the very essence of collective deterrence and defense. Had the United Nations possessed such a capability in the summer of 1990, and had the Security Council deployed it to Kuwait as a tripwire, it is extremely doubtful that Iraq would have actually invaded that country. Once the conflict with Iraq was under way, elements of the NATO AMF were in fact deployed to eastern Turkey, as the member of the Alliance in potential danger, for precisely that purpose.

The land component of the AMF, comprised of an international staff headquarters and designated battalions from a majority of Alliance members, constitutes a 5,000-6,000 man brigade group with artillery and combat support. Air squadrons are assigned to support the AMF as needed and are commanded by the NATO Air Force commander in the region concerned. The entire force is trained and tested in annual exercises on both the northern and southern flanks of ACE. In 1993, it will be renamed the Immediate Reaction Force, backed up by Rapid Reaction Corps which will be analogous to a UN Quick Reaction Force such as we have proposed.

The present AMF is essentially the model we have in mind for the UN Legion in its start-up phase except that combat elements would be under UN command and control at all times and that the ground forces would be integrated at the individual level instead of as national companies or battalions. As in the case of NATO's AMF, the need for frequent and realistic exercises and evaluations is obvious.

At the December 1967 Ministerial Meeting of the North Atlantic Council, the decision was made to form a permanent multinational squadron of destroyers and frigates for service in the North Atlantic -- to be, in effect, a naval counterpart to the ACE Mobile Force. When the first squadron of the Standing Naval Force Atlantic (STANAVFORLANT or "SNFA") sailed from the United Kingdom in January 1965, a multinational force was permanently deployed at sea to demonstrate for the first time in modern naval history.

Growing out of the interest in NATO's proposed Multilateral Force and the new strategic emphasis on "flexible response," the SNFA served as a practical demonstration of the seapower potential and political solidarity of the Alliance. In 1993 STANAVFORLANT will celebrate its 25th Anniversary. More than 580 NATO ships and some 150,000 men and women will have served in one way or another in the unique squadron. The Force has participated in more than 150 NATO maritime operations or exercises and contributed to NATO's success in changing the world's political scenario.[11]

The NATO members that permanently contribute one or more warships to the Force are Canada, Germany, Netherlands, United Kingdom and United States. Denmark, Norway, Portugal and Spain have contributed warships periodically. Thus, nine of the sixteen NATO members have participated in the Force.

Operating jointly calls for one working language and an organization with fully integrated staff work. All the national participants have to share and even modify their respective national procedures and to accept a common identity. For example, warships of the SNFA fly the NATO flag on the starboard yardarm and show the NATO emblem on both sides of each ship's funnel to demonstrate that the deployment is part of an alliance mission under SACLANT.

In April 1992, the Allied Naval Forces "on-call" in the Mediterranean became the "Standing Naval Force Mediterranean." Permanently contributing members are: France, Germany, Greece, Italy, Netherlands,

Turkey, United Kingdom and United States. The first operational assignment of the eight nation fleet was to take station off the coast of the former Yugoslavia where, under the NATO flag and as a "Regional Agency," they assist the United Nations pursuant to Chapter VIII of the Charter with the peacekeeping efforts among former Yugoslavian republics and monitor the sanctions against Serbia.

There has also been a Standing Naval Force Channel since 1973 which is under the command of NATO's CINCHAN. A major value of these forces, whether on-call or standing is the training they give national navies in operating together, an experience which has proved beneficial in the Persian Gulf both at the time of the Iran-Iraq War (when European elements drawn from NATO were coordinated by the Western European Union) and in Desert Shield/Storm.

The Proposed Multilateral Force (MLF)

In its day, the proposal for a NATO MLF was sometimes headline news and a source of controversy within the Alliance and in East-West relations.[12] Voluminous writings debated this proposed method of "sharing" nuclear weapons among the allies. It sought to give them and especially Germany and Italy a role in nuclear deterrence without violating nonproliferation obligations. Eventually, however, the Non-Proliferation Treaty effectively barred the MLF, which also failed owing to insufficient political support in Europe and U.S. Congressional opposition.

It was eventually supplanted by the NATO Nuclear Planning Group which aimed at sharing responsibility for plans and policy rather than hardware. All of that is now merely a footnote to history. But even at the mid-sixties height of the debates, little attention was paid to the innovative thinking that went into what would have been something new under the sun: a commonly owned and operated international military enterprise with a legal personality distinct from that of the states participating in the force. This distinctive character is the valuable legacy for UN consideration, rather than the policy issue of nuclear sharing or the perceived need for an "allied" nuclear deterrent over and above that possessed by the United States and Britain (and later, France).

"NATO's nuclear dilemma," as it was then termed, was how to meet the dangers of Soviet nuclear blackmail of continental Europe while combining triggers with safety catches. This very real problem drove the staff work among eight alliance members for several years during the presidencies of Dwight Eisenhower, John F. Kennedy and Lyndon B. Johnson.

The records of the MLF Working Group and its military, legal and technical subgroups comprise cubic yards of material. A set is available to scholars at the Hoover Institution in Palo Alto, California. This documentation, plus personal diaries, formed the basis for the doctoral dissertation of one of this book's authors which is the primary source for this section.[13]

The MLF was, of course, a nuclear deterrent force only. Once proposed for Polaris submarines, it evolved (after objections from Admiral Rickover and other U.S. nuclear submariners) into plans for small surface warships as platforms. Lacking much defensive armament, these ships would depend on their mobility and on blending in with the hundreds of merchant ships plying the same waters daily to escape detection and pre-emptive targeting.

In its later stages, consideration was also given to manned nuclear strike aircraft and even surface-to-surface Pershing missiles. Admittedly, its weapons systems, security and command and control problems and cost estimates have little applicability to other international forces, such as those proposed for the UN in this book. But in legal, administrative and personnel aspects and overall concept terms, the parallels are many and instructive.

Perhaps the best way to summarize the ground-breaking nature of the work done on the MLF is to review the draft of an "Atlantic Nuclear Defense Community" which would have governed the MLF or ("Force"). The draft drew on the work of the five sub-groups (Military, Legal, Security and Safety, Financial and Administrative) established by the MLF Working Group in Paris and was compiled by its Secretariat and Principal Secretary.[14]

The Community was to act in its own name, operate a common Force, including warships under a distinctive flag, and own all military equipment. The parties would be individually and collectively responsible for the Community which was to abide by and be entitled to the protection of applicable rules of international law. As an armed force of all the participants, the Force was to be used only for defense in accord with the UN Charter and any attack on it would be an attack against each of the parties.

The Community was to have a Board of Governors with a rotating chairmanship, composed of one representative (normally a NATO Permanent Representative) from each party which could be empowered to decide and act on all Community matters, to promulgate rules, approve budgets and delegate authority.

The Board was to act by an affirmative vote of two-thirds of its members, except for decisions to employ (or release to SACEUR) nuclear weapons, which would require an affirmative vote by "Europe" and by the United States. The Board's analogous entity in the United Nations would be the Security Council. (In the absence of a European union, European parties with over 40 million in population had four votes each, those with 10-40 million had two votes, and others one. Eight such weighted votes (from countries representing at least 12 votes) would constitute an affirmative vote for Europe.)

The Board would appoint (and could dismiss) a Director-General as chief executive of the Community in charge of personnel, administration, finance and procurement and of liaison with NATO and other international organizations. He was to have an integrated civilian and military headquarters staff and would be comparable to the UN (or NATO) Secretary-General.

The Board would also appoint a Force Commander under the authority of the Director-General with a staff to assist him in his responsibilities for the command, administration and logistic support of operating units and military installations. The Commander would maintain the essential military liaison with SACEUR and with national military authorities. (This Commander would have as a UN counterpart the proposed Chief of Staff under the Secretary-General.)

The Force itself would have an initial military component, intended to be four U.S. nuclear submarines (until they were eliminated from the planning), 20 surface warships with a combined total of 126 missiles, and 64 British bombers. Subsequent components could be added and the weapons systems changed or upgraded by affirmative U.S. and European votes.

All elements of the Community were specified in the charter to be "staffed and manned throughout in an integrated manner by a mixture of nationals of the parties," in rough proportion to the total personnel from each participant. Weapons-related functions could have no more than 40% of the personnel from nationals of any one party. No military component was to operate without participation of at least three parties, and each party was to join at least one component.

Membership in the Community would be open to all other NATO members and it was to function within the NATO framework, including assignment of the Force to SACEUR. Its security and safety controls were to be no less stringent than those of parties supplying nuclear warheads.

Both civilian and military personnel were to be from participants only and responsible solely to the Community without external instructions, and all would be paid by the Community -- not countries -- on a uniform scale under Board regulations. Military personnel were to be selected by the Director General (not the Commander) from candidates nominated by the parties.

There was to be a distinct Community military personnel system, compatible where possible with those of the parties, and military personnel would wear the uniform of the Community -- another lesson for any UN standing force.

However, because of special concerns about the applicability of the Geneva Conventions (e.g. on treatment of POWs), Community military personnel were also to retain rights and obligations, including promotional opportunities and retirement, as members of their national armed services under their national law. Such dual status, some felt, would run counter to the international service principles underlying the charter, and it proved to be a difficult issue.

Other provisions of the Charter dealt with military discipline (a special Board regulation was to be issued on rights and obligations of personnel), procurement and supply, normally to be conducted through the appropriate governmental agencies of the parties, and finance.

The common costs for other than military components were to be apportioned by the Board, with no one party bearing over 40%, while the military component costs were to be shared only among parties which participated in that specific component. Countries in serious arrears on financial obligations could be denied voting rights. Detailed financial regulations, of which an experts' draft had been prepared, were to be issued by the Board.

The draft charter concluded with normal treaty provisions for entry into force, review and amendment. Duration would be indefinite with no right of withdrawal until dissolution by the Board, when assets would be divided pro rata except for missile and warhead returns to the supplying party. Depository arrangements and registry with the United Nations were specified. Two special provisions were declarations of consistency with other international engagements and an undertaking not to enter into conflicting engagements, including arms control, unless the Community as a whole subscribed to them; and incorporation by reference into the Community's governance of agreements to be made on status of forces and personnel; on claims (with an independent community Tribunal) and on the initial military component.

On the thorny issue of military discipline, the general scheme distinguished between minor offenses and breaches of discipline for which commanding officers could impose minor fines and restrictions, usually with the concurrence of the senior available officer of the offender's nationality; and major offenses, such as mutiny, assault on officers, or gross breaches of security, where trial and punishment were to be referred to the offender's national armed forces. Some similar approach might have to be developed for the United Nations Legion, but with greater disciplinary authority for the Legion itself.

Could the scheme of the charter have worked in practice? In the opinion of the authors, all three of whom worked on aspects of the MLF proposal, the answer is probably yes -- provided that the political levels of participating governments were willing to sign and implement the key documents. The proposal became moot before that point was reached, although there was plenty of political input, often from quite high policy levels, as well as that from national experts, to developing the concepts and documents involved.

Could the operational aspects have been developed successfully? Here there is more empirical evidence, especially on the feasibility of mixed manning. Initiated at the suggestion of President Kennedy, an 18-month experiment (officially termed a demonstration) was conducted aboard the U.S. destroyer *Biddle* (DG-5) armed with surface to air missiles and ASW weapons.

Renamed the U.S.S. *Claude B. Ricketts* in honor of the American Admiral who had helped pioneer the MLF proposal, the demonstration got under way in May 1964 with a crew of 10 American officers and 164 men, and 10 allied officers and 162 men of British, Dutch, German, Greek, Italian and

Turkish nationality. Monitored carefully by a naval committee from their countries, the demonstration was evaluated as a success, and the *Ricketts* operated well as an element of the U.S. Atlantic Fleet in NATO exercises.[15]

Many of the lessons learned were incorporated into the draft MLF charter and related documents discussed above, such as the importance of fluency in a common language (and special remedial training where warranted); the need for a common and distinctive uniform and insignia; the importance of equal pay, the sensitivity to cultural, culinary, recreational and religious preferences; and the need for command discipline authority. Not a few of these findings seem applicable to any proposed UN standing force or Legion and jibe also with the Franco-German brigade experience discussed earlier.

Above all, the demonstration and the entire MLF experience show that able, dedicated, and ambitious career military personnel can be attracted to the ideal of international service and can perform as an integrated unit at least as well as their compatriots in national armed services.

Part III: Starting Up The UN Legion

The lessons we have highlighted in this chapter drawn from the UN itself, from NATO and the MLF and the Franco-German experiment support the book's recommendations for a revamped UN peace and security system, to include a standing and truly international UN Legion. While these lessons also suggest that such a force is feasible, it is bound to encounter significant problems and to generate controversy.

There can be no certainty that the system would work until it has been tried and proven under actual UN auspices. Consequently, we have recommended that it be initiated on an experimental basis with an inaugural phase limited to a single enhanced brigade, approximately the ground strength of NATO's Mobile Force. To get started, it might be necessary to use carefully selected personnel detailed from participating countries who would serve as the initial training cadre and form the peacekeeping or enforcement elements should the Legion have to be deployed in a crisis before it was permanently established. To initiate the mixed manning, all such personnel would have to know two languages, one of them English.

In a press interview at the time of his June 1992 "An Agenda for

Peace" proposal, Secretary-General Boutros-Ghali told a reporter that he would ask as many countries as possible "to let me have up to 1,000 trained troops within 24 hours."[16] (Such a 1,000 man peacekeeping contingent had in fact been offered by French President Mitterand at the January Summit session of the Security Council.)

However, without infrastructure, command-control-communications (C3) and staff organization, fifteen groups (from the Security Council members alone) of 1,000 men each would be little more than an armed mob! Moreover, they would be available only on-call and would not be a standing force training and working together. We would therefore seek instead company-sized detachments to be detailed to the Legion from those countries (and others) for the initial phase. Perhaps one country with an outstanding record in peacekeeping, such as Canada or one of the Nordic group would offer a base and initial logistic support during the inaugural phase -- analogous, in a way, to the mixed-manning demonstration held for the MLF aboard the U.S.S. *Ricketts*. But in this case, the "host" should not be the U.S.A. or any other permanent Security Council member.

However, a Legion Commander, Chief of Staff, and headquarters staff should be appointed at the outset from seconded volunteers of outstanding ability. One of their vital initial tasks would be to recommend (from existing weapons and supplies and surplus stocks when possible) the common personal and unit equipment, including air transportable tanks, artillery and other vehicles and weapons for the Legion TO&E (Table of Organization and Equipment) as the unit develops. New designs or procurement from manufacturers should be avoided for reasons of both cost and time.

The UN Secretariat and the embryo Military Staff would also need a few full-time civilian and military personnel at UN Headquarters to help with recruiting, finance, logistics and administrative problems, ranging from design of a common uniform to personnel and disciplinary procedures, legal questions and the like. One senior person, selected by the Secretary-General, should head this Legion support group with the simple mission: "Do everything necessary to make it happen!" He and the Legion Commander would have to work as a team, one in the field and one at UN headquarters.

The Legion support staff would also need guidance from countries in the course of this work, and the Peace Management Committee we have recommended, or a subcommittee, could serve that purpose. It would have a role analogous to that of the MLF Working Group which did the preparatory work for that proposed novel force.

During an interim phase the Legion would begin to recruit and train individual volunteers, even while having some combat-capable elements composed of the inaugural units mentioned above. Assuming that evaluation by military staff in the participating countries and in the Legion itself was positive after, say 18 months of start-up and experimentation, the final phase would begin under Security Council re-authorization.

This would involve the staffing, equipping and financing (see Chapter Six) of the Legion on a truly multilateral basis and the preparation of permanent facilities. The initial detailed forces would be phased out. After another year and a half of integrated training, the Legion should be ready for action and for decisions on whether to enlarge the inaugural force and expand its location geographically, as well as how best to provide permanent air and naval support. By then, it is hoped, other elements of the UN system would be in place, including the Chief of Staff, Military Staff, Secretariat improvements, and meaningful Article 43 inventories and commitments, including Quick Reaction Forces. Also at this point, decisions can be made about how best to organize and train troops for both peacekeeping and peace-enforcement missions so that they can be used in either role as situations require on a cost-effective basis.

While there will always be professional doubters, and objections to the Legion's cost will be raised, we believe that once a "United Nations Legion" is in being, it will attract widespread media and public interest and support around the world. Politicians will take pride in "their" world force -- just as the U.S. Marines have sometimes been called "Congress's Own Troops." Here, even the smallest countries will see in the Legion a symbol of a new United Nations and an independent military element not entirely controlled by the large powers.

The momentum should build on itself, assuming careful planning and management from the outset. The problem, then, is to get started. The authors hope these suggestions will help.

CHAPTER FIVE

THE SYSTEM AT WORK
APPLYING THE PROPOSED MODEL: YUGOSLAVIA

The functioning of the UN system proposed in this book can be illustrated by a hypothetical case, based for realism on the current breakup of Yugoslavia; but it is not an analysis of that actual problem. Instead, the hypothesis is intended to show how the UN could deal with the disintegration of Yugoslavia were it taking place generally along the lines of the current situation but several years after the UN had adopted the recommendations herein, and had successfully accomplished the great and time-consuming tasks of making the revised system effective.

Anticipation

A recognized problem of the existing UN is its limited ability to anticipate problems. Under the revised system, however, the first stirring of movement toward independence in Slovenia and Croatia would generate an organized analysis of the situation on both the political and military sides of the UN. The Secretariat would obtain information from its own resources, from member nations, and from observers, and would draw on members for analytical expertise and local knowledge. The political analysis would forecast the development of the situation, within Yugoslavia and in the attitudes and concerns of other nations, and it would calculate the costs and political impacts of various UN actions. The military analysis would examine the forces in Yugoslavia and estimate the outcomes of various conflicts there; it would judge the forces and resources that the UN would require for each of the missions that the Security Council might assign; and it would consider who might best provide them, and how long it would take to have them deployed.

These analyses would be refined and updated continuously and provide the data for the Secretary-General to make early and repeated reports to the Security Council under Article 99. They would constitute the bases for decisions by the Security Council and the Peace Management Committee (PMC), for positions taken by member nations, and for preparations by the Secretary-General.

Execution

The Yugoslav breakup would present a spectrum of actions that the UN might take, and a decision to take any one of them could be changed as events and judgements dictated. UN preparations and actions, therefore, even after the Security Council had directed a specific course, would need to include a running analysis of the effects of decisions and be prepared for resulting changes in the composition and operations of UN forces. The spectrum of possibilities in the Yugoslav case would include the following five hypothetical scenarios.

Case 1: Watching Brief

A UN determination that the Yugoslav situation was a civil war, an internal problem, and UN action was not indicated.

Case 2: Mediation and Peacekeeping

A determination by the United Nations, especially assuming that much of the international community recognized the independence of Slovenia, Croatia, Bosnia, Macedonia, and others, that an international dispute existed which called for pacific settlement under Chapter VI of the Charter.

In the latter case, the UN would send negotiators to try to arrange cease-fires, organize a peacekeeping force and, when the force was ready and at least a semblance of cease-fire was in effect, dispatch the peacekeeping force for consensual, neutral peacekeeping.

The peacekeeping force would be created essentially under the existing system. However, the Secretary-General's expanded military organization would be able to contribute in a number of ways, particularly in anticipating the possibility of a shift, in whole or in part, to Chapter VII operations where UN forces would be employed to threaten or execute enforcement measures. This could put the UN in armed conflict with Serbia, and destroy the neutrality of the UN peacekeepers. The peacekeepers would then be regarded by Serbia as hostile forces subject to attack. Allowing for such possibility would influence the numbers and armament of peacekeeping troops, their stationing, the plans for responding to attack, and the readying of relief forces for them if needed.

Presumably the number and locations of the peacekeepers in Slovenia and Croatia would be more or less as at present. Bosnia would call for a similar force, probably centered on Sarajevo. Extensions of the hostilities to other former provinces would add to the need. A total peacekeeping force could run to 30,000 or even more, largely infantry battalions. They would be drawn from member nations whose neutrality was credible, and not include elements from those Security Council/PMC nations who would provide the Quick Reaction Forces if enforcement operations were ordered.

Preparatory measures for the peacekeeping forces would be undertaken while the Security Council was arriving at a decision to deploy them, and go forward urgently while the Secretary-General was negotiating a cease-fire. The UN field commander and staff would be selected and equipped; arrangements would be made with nations agreeing to supplying troops, facilities, transportation, and resources; and advance parties would be established in the critical area to establish communications and select bases and deployment sites.

When the order to deploy was given, the peacekeepers should be able to move into position promptly, on a schedule dictated largely by transportation times. Yugoslavia is accessible by sea, land, and air; first elements could arrive quickly if necessary.

Case 3: Humanitarian Protection

A determination by the United Nations that a humanitarian requirement or other localized situation demanded a limited, specific combat operation. The current example would be the relief of a siege of Sarajevo. That could well develop as a Chapter "VI and 3/4" operation. That is, while establishing control of the airhead centered on Sarajevo airport and the ground communications from Split and perhaps Dubrovnik on the Adriatic could require combat operations, it need not necessarily be interpreted as hostilities between the UN and Serbia. Serbia could take the position that the besieging forces were not hers but those of Serbian inhabitants of Bosnia; the UN could emphasize that its enforcement actions were local and that its peacekeepers remained neutral. Both sides could see advantages in maintaining those positions.

Even the limited relief expedition, however, would be a major operation. The mission would be to control a UN airhead with a radius of 20 miles from the Sarajevo airport, including the city, and to establish ground communications from the Adriatic coast. Planners would have to assume that the UN forces would encounter powerful Serbian opposition and that they would face missile and artillery antiaircraft defenses and encounter mortar and artillery fire from the hills surrounding city and airport. They should also expect attacks by Serb forces possibly with some armor and artillery, on the roads from airport to city and airport to Adriatic. They would have to deal with counterattacks by guerrillas or Serb forces throughout the airhead, and expect large numbers of snipers in the city and countryside, where virtually every male is armed. Other ethnic irregulars could also cause problems. There could be some Serbian air opposition. Even after the UN had established itself in the city, in the airhead, and on the roads, it could expect attacks by Serbian troops that could infiltrate the airhead and city and attack movement along the routes.

UN operations would require a campaign to insure air supremacy, to suppress Serb ground-to-air missiles and AA artillery threatening the air approaches to the airport, and to minimize the artillery and mortar fire on the airport or radar-controlled ground artillery could help to suppress the hostile fire. This would clear the way for intervention by a corps of airborne and air-transported ground forces, who would seize the airport and then establish control of the road to the city, of the city itself, and of the airhead.

During the air preparation, a support base would be established in Split and a brigade of the UN Legion could be deployed there. As soon as the Sarajevo airfield was secured, truck convoys escorted by these ground troops and covered by ground support aircraft or helicopter gunships would start making the 125 mile run through the mountains from Split to Sarajevo, opening and maintaining that major supply line.

The Force Commander and Staff and Air Component Commander and Staff would be chosen and equipped as early as possible. It would be essential that these commanders and the bulk of their staffs be thoroughly familiar with the UN operational doctrines and methods that would by then have been developed for UN forces and tested and refined in international exercises. The necessary equipment, especially for communications and transportation from member nations would have to be on hand. The commanders would be established initially on a major airbase at Foggia in southeastern Italy, and deployed forward to Sarajevo as soon as the airfield was secured. The Force Commander would retain direct control of the ground component, and exercise his air control through the Air Component Commander (ACC). The latter would establish and operate the Air Operations Center. All suppliers of air elements would have representatives in the AOC and report their availabilities and requirements there. The ACC would assign missions and schedules and prescribe coordination -- effectively controlling all air operations. Ground coordination would be accomplished largely by the assignment of sectors to national elements.

Ground forces might consist of a corps of three divisions and, possibly, a brigade of the UN Legion, whose soldiers could come from as many as 60 different countries. The corps could consist of one Russian airborne division (with an airborne or seaborne tail to provide mobility) and one air transportable division each from Germany (assuming necessary changes in German law) and France.

Tactical aviation could be provided by the UK, the U.S., and France, utilizing bases in Germany and Italy as well as Sarajevo. Airlift would come largely from the U.S. and Russia.

Nations would be responsible for providing logistic support to their national elements. Agreements for cross-supply could be negotiated between nations. Some common elements would be centrally supplied. For example, Saudi Arabia could furnish fuel and oil (POL).

UN forces directly involved in this operation would add up to some 50-60,000 ground troops, plus tactical, troop carrier, and transport air elements. Depending on the effectiveness of preparations made during the UN's discussion phase, the initial landings on the Sarajevo airstrip should be made four to six weeks after the Security Council decision. Shortly thereafter, the mission of the force should be successfully achieved, i.e. the city should be largely freed from artillery, mortar, and sniper fire, and should be receiving sufficient supplies to sustain it. The end of the operation, however, would depend on the determination of the Serbians; UN actions within the airhead would not defeat Serbian forces beyond the periphery, and they would retain the capacity to continue attacks and infiltrations there, or elsewhere.

Case 4: Security Enforcement

A determination by the United Nations that Serbian actions constituted aggression and required military action under Article 42 of Chapter VII to restore international peace and security. This would be a directive for a major campaign and a declaration of conflict by the world community with Serbia and those elements of the former Yugoslavia that adhered to Serbia. They would probably include Montenegro and ethnically Serbian populations in Slovenia, Croatia, Bosnia-Herzegovina, and elsewhere.

The Security Council could assign any of three missions to the UN force: first, to end the fighting, that is, to engage Serbian forces where they were operating and stop them there, leaving the boundaries between the combatants where the fighting ended; or second, to restore the boundaries of the ex-Yugoslavian states as they existed before their declarations of independence, driving the Serbian forces out of the areas they had overrun; or, third, to defeat the Serbian forces and make their leaders sue for peace. Neither of the first two would effectively discharge the objective, of restoring peace and security, and hostile forces of ancient enemies would be left facing one another across hotly disputed boundaries. Only the third would produce a stable outcome -- or as nearly stable as is achievable in that ever-smoldering area. The third might therefore be chosen.

Carrying out such a full-scale combat operation would be an exacting test of the UN's newly developed organization. The UN Military Staff should have developed a concept of operations for the Secretary-General's approval and clearance with the Security Council during the Council's discussion phase. That concept would be the basis for designating the Field Commander and his principal subordinates (notably the Air Component Commander), assembling and equipping their staffs, and deploying them to advance Headquarters from which to prepare and conduct the initial operations. The staff concept would also permit blocking out the forces and support resources to be needed (subject to modification as the Force Commander's Operation Plan took shape), determining who should best provide them (largely but not exclusively from earmarked Quick Action Forces) and getting agreement from the countries involved. The nations concerned would then be able to go ahead with preparing their forces, arranging their support, and deploying them to meet the Force Commander's plan.

The Force Commander's plan would specify the operations to be conducted, their timing and their objectives. The objectives would depend on how the situation developed during the preparatory phase. It is possible that just the existence of the powerful UN buildup would be enough to persuade the Serbian authorities to cede; or perhaps the impact of the initial ground/air assaults would be adequate. If Serbia continued its aggression, however, the full operation would be required, supplemented by embargo and blockade measures.

The Force Commander might make the taking of Belgrade, with the seat of government his major initial objective, and launch these operations:

• An air campaign to establish air supremacy, and to the degree possible immobilize the Serbian forces and destroy their heavy weapons and transport.

• An armored/mechanized air/ground thrust assembling in Hungary south of Budapest, crossing into ex-Yugoslavia at Szeged-Subotica and driving direct to Belgrade some 150 miles down the relatively flat Tisa (Theiss) and Danube valleys. The ground elements could be based on two divisions each from Russia and Germany, and those countries would also provide the bulk of the tactical air support for this drive.

• A ground/air thrust to clear Slovenia and Croatia and to open the operational and supply routes for elements brought by sea. This force would assemble at Rijeka (Fiume) or, if Rijeka was in Serbian hands, at Trieste, and proceed through the mountains along the road/rail communications to Zagreb (115 miles) and thence to Belgrade (250 miles), joining the first thrust. Facing the mountainous terrain, the ground forces would be lighter -- one motorized division each from the U.S. and the major west European countries -- and if substantially challenged they would need powerful air support principally from those nations.

• A number of supporting actions would be undertaken: establishing control of the Adriatic by the (NATO) Standing Naval Force Mediterranean led by the Italian Navy to preclude attacks on UN shipping or sea support of Serbian forces; securing the coastal cities, especially Split and Dubrovnik, to be ready to push an attack through to Sarajevo when the situation indicated using the UN Legion, reinforced, if necessary, by the Sixth Fleet's amphibious task group with its embarked Marine brigade; and arranging for Greece, Bulgaria, Romania, Hungary, and Austria to guard their borders tightly to prevent support of Serbia from their territories.

• Subsequent operations would depend on the way the situation developed. It might be necessary to deal with remaining regular forces in the south and the southeast, notably Bosnia-Herzegovina.

• Continuing anti-guerrilla operations might be required.

Case 5: Hostilities

Hostilities against Serbia could be on a scale comparable to that of Desert Storm, which called for half a million men and required five months preparation before the attack was launched, even with the advantages of having a commander and staff who had been studying, reconnoitering, and developing plans for the theater for years, and having a command structure set up to support them with which they had long worked. Similarly, a substantial readying time would be essential for the UN attack against Serbia; it would be ill-advised in the extreme to launch a Serbian "war" with inadequate force or hasty preparation. Failure would be a disaster not only for the Balkans, but for the whole concept of collective action by the UN to enforce peace and security. Given reasonably adequate performance by the UN political and military system, however, the outcome would not be in doubt, and the prestige of the UN and the potency of its resolutions in subsequent cases should be mightily enhanced. But as we have noted earlier, persistence even in the face of set-backs and over a long period of time would be required both by the UN organization and those Security Council and other members taking part in the fighting.

In such complex scenarios, it is hard to fix a specific mission for the UN Legion. It could be part of the early peacekeeping deployment so as to be "dual capable" if events forced it into an enforcement role. Or it could be the lead element in a larger effort to force entry into Sarajevo. Finally, it could be part of a preventive deployment to a nearby staging base early in the crisis to show the parties that the UN was serious about using force if diplomatic efforts failed and civilian populations were placed at risk. It is the flexibility of such an international brigade that makes it a potentially invaluable resource at the Security Council's disposal. For cases 4 and 5, however, the Legion would be subsumed into the much larger operations carried out with the national forces that had been assigned to UN duties. In those circumstances, the Security Council might decide to withdraw the Legion to hold it in reserve for contingencies that might develop simultaneously in other parts of the world. The preoccupation of the UN and major powers with the postulated Serbian conflict might even encourage aggression elsewhere, so that the peace and security system must be strong enough to cope with two major and several minor threats to the peace simultaneously.

CHAPTER SIX

FINANCING UN FORCES

The UN's Financial Crisis

United Nations financing is a labyrinth that even experts enter with trepidation. One does not have to be an expert, however, to realize that the UN is in a grave and worsening crisis as its members add new missions at an unprecedented rate without a concomitant willingness to pay for them, or even to settle their past obligations to the organization, (As of March 1992, some 150 countries owed $1.8 billion in unpaid regular and special assessments of which the U.S. owed over 40%)[1].

Former Secretary-General Perez de Cuellar warned of a coming disaster in the fall of 1991. His successor, Boutros-Ghali spoke of a chasm between ends and means, saying: "our vision cannot really extend to the prospect opening before us as long as our financing remains myopic."[2]

The United Nations has two primary budgets, a regular one covering the costs of the organization itself -- but not of the specialized agencies, which have their own finances, and a separate one for peacekeeping which has financed virtually all of the missions discussed in Chapter Four. There is thus far no provision at all for financing peace-enforcement, since the major costs of Korea and the Gulf coalition were handled by the United States and others outside the UN system.

The UN's regular budget for 1992 is just over $1 billion and the peacekeeping budget about $2.7 billion. As noted, many countries, including the United States, are in arrears for both budgets for past years as well as the current one. The UN's regular scale of assessment, or apportionment, is determined by the General Assembly, as required by Article 17 of the Charter and is renegotiated every three years, most recently in 1991.[3]

In principle, shares are proportional to a country's Gross National Product; but special provisions apply to the poorer members and many pay the minimum of .01%; and there is an upper limit of 25%, which only the U.S. pays. (Japan is the next highest at 11.4% followed by Russia at 10% and Germany at 9.4%) A fair case can be made that Germany, Japan and others should pick up another two or three per cent between them and allow the U.S. a reduction if and as Russia regains an ability to pay in hard currency.

A special scale applies to peacekeeping operations, broken down by groups of countries. Permanent Security Council members pay more than they would under the regular scale but range from under 1% for China to Britain and France's 5-6%, Russia's 9.4% and the U.S. share of over 30%. While industrialized states pay the same as their regular budget share, the wealthier developing countries are liable for only a fifth of that rate, which is manifestly too low, since they are the most likely beneficiaries of UN peacekeeping. The poorest are assessed at merely one tenth of the regular scale, or as little as $5,000 each,[4] barely enough to pay one peacekeeper for 5 months at the minimum rate. All of the 78 least developed countries together could finance at best one platoon a year with their peacekeeping dues.

There is also a UN Working Capital Fund of $100 million, proposed to be doubled, which is used mainly to cover cash flow problems from delayed dues payments and unforeseen contingencies. The current Secretary-General and his predecessor have proposed a standby Peacekeeping Reserve Fund for start-up costs and an interest-earning $1 billion UN Peace Endowment Fund which have yet to be acted upon. The Endowment goal seems modest in the light of current peacekeeping costs which will run to at least that amount per year in both Cambodia and the former Yugoslavia. While the UN did once issue special bonds, bought by governments, to overcome the financial impasse brought on by the Congo crisis,[5] the Secretary-General has usually been denied borrowing authority. Even the ability of the UN to charge interest on overdue assessments has not been granted by the General Assembly.

The UN is at the mercy of its members' financial straits and whims and budget cycles. For instance, the U.S. pays at the end of its fiscal year in October, although assessments are payable at the beginning of the calendar year. Thus, the UN has literally lived hand to mouth and survived by robbing Peter to pay Paul. Now both Peter and Paul (the regular and peacekeeping budgets) are broke, and the UN's Working Capital Fund of $100 million has been drawn down and not yet replenished.

Before turning to potential ways out of the maze, we must further complicate it by evaluating the costs of the enhanced peace and security system.

Costs of the Proposed UN Peace and Security System

We are treating peacekeeping costs as an on-going element of the system to be financed from the peacekeeping assessment, but with the changes as discussed below and with the flexibility to accommodate to new demands as needed.

Many nations have expressed concern over the efficiency and cost-effectiveness of the procedures by which the Secretariat and Force Commanders meet their operational expenses.[6] Nordic countries have proposed training programs for senior peacekeeping personnel to allow greater financial and administrative responsibility for Force Commanders (or Special UN Representatives) and a reduction in the duplication of civilian and military staff functions.

Peacekeeping will continue to be the organization's most expensive and highest profile regular activity. The UN must therefore restructure its ad hoc system even as it struggles to obtain adequate resources. Many countries have invested much thought and planning into their contributions. The Scandinavian group in particular has coordinated training and doctrine, standardized organization and equipment and offered ready on-call forces. Their peacekeeping manual, formally called "Nordic UN Stand-By Forces" should be a model for other peacekeeping contributors. But relatively little has been done to turn this excellent beginning into UN standard operating procedure. So there is much to be done on the cost-effectiveness side as well as in regard to revenue. We assume that, one way or another, current peacekeeping budgets of $2.7 billion can be met and we note that as this book goes to press, the U.S. Congress is considering bills to fund the American share.[7]

The headquarters costs of the enhanced system we propose would be mainly for the augmentation of the Secretariat for crisis management and the establishment of an adequate situation room. The few additional spaces, which should not be over 20-25, could probably be found during the current restructuring of the existing staff; if not, including them should not require more than one to two million dollars a year. The main cost would be the creation of the UN Military Staff of at least 200 military officers. We believe they should be international military servants, and like their civil counterparts be paid by the UN rather than by governments, to enhance their objectivity.

A ball park estimate for such a staff and the necessary office and communications equipment would be on the order of $20 million for personnel (assuming an annual per man total cost, with clerical support, of $100,000) and another $10-$20 million for special equipment, communications, and other operational requirements. (This cost would be lower once the systems were in place.) This is in line with recommendations by a group of experts to create "United Nations Security Forces."[8] Their proposal envisages not only a central civilian and military headquarters staff analogous to what we are suggesting, but also a permanent, central UN command, three regional command staffs in nucleus or cadre form and four embryo staffs for special alert and maritime elements. They estimate total annual costs of U.S. $40 million for organization, infrastructure and a total of 300 personnel.

For reasons described earlier, including the unpredictability of the contingencies a new UN system might have to face, we do not recommend standing regional or functional UN commands in addition to the headquarters military staff, which in our scheme would help establish field commands as needed. Thus it would appear that $40-$50 million per year would be adequate for the purpose.

The UN Legion is harder to cost, for it depends critically on certain assumptions. We assume that in the start-up, costs could be minimized by: (1) donation of base facilities for training; (2) gradual phasing in of the individual volunteers with an initial cadre furnished by no-cost contributions of company-sized detachments from the countries serving on the Peace Management Committee; (3) use of existing equipment purchased at a discount from unused surpluses or donated by countries. In the initial orientation and training phase, a full set of combat equipment should not be needed.

In the United States, the defense dollar is spent roughly one third for procurement, including R&D and testing; one third for operations and maintenance and one third for military personnel (29%) and other (4%).

Included are civilian personnel expenses and accrual costs for military retirement pay.[9]

For the second phase of the Legion, with one full brigade as discussed earlier, the principal costs would also fall into these categories, plus a factor for base overhead and construction, if needed, rations, recreation and medical benefits, and an allowance for airlift to overseas training exercises.

Using U.S. cost figures can be misleading. If one divides total Army personnel into the total budget for that service, the cost per man can exceed $100,000. But this includes procurement, R&D, overhead, and intelligence and other support. The actual annual personnel costs for all ranks (including officers) with several years service is closer to $40,000.

The United Nations own peacekeeping forces appear to cost about $35,000 to $45,000 per man based upon, for example, the Protection Force in Yugoslavia or the advance mission in Cambodia. These have civilian and police as well as military elements and include UN equipment, food, housing and transportation; but military pay is at the minimum UN rate, discussed below.[10]

Estimating pay costs for the Legion again requires some assumptions: Are they paid at U.S. rates? UN reimbursement scales? An average of developed and developing country rates? Our strong recommendation, based upon extensive study for NATO's Multilateral Force, is that all personnel of a given rank or rating receive uniform amounts on payday. For it seems essential for morale that men serving together in an integrated unit have equivalent purchasing power available to them. Competing considerations are that no one's total compensation should be lower than that of his colleagues in national service; that the "windfall" to the lowest paid soldiers not appear excessive; and that military personnel costs be affordable in the UN context.

One way to balance these factors is to have a high uniform rate, calculated, say as an average for the NATO countries. Those whose countries pay more would have the differential paid into a home bank account for their (or their dependents') use. Countries paying far less could have an option of imposing a special tax rate on the windfall portion, adjusted for the soldier's cost of living at his post. But the principle should remain equal pay for equal work, rank and risks, with enough incentive to attract the best volunteers for what could easily be hazardous duty.

It seems reasonable to use a Legion personnel cost of $30,000 per man.

(The relatively few who who would get more through differential allowances would add only 2 or 3 million dollars a year.) So personnel for the 5,000 man one-brigade Legion would be about $150 million.

For other cost components we have averaged figures for Legion-sized elements from the equipment-light 7th Infantry Division with its air mobility and helicopter support and from the 101st Airborne Division. Operations and maintenance might be $40 million annually on this basis. The annualized portion of U.S. TO&E procurement varies widely by type of unit and estimated useful life. A round figure of $100 million seems reasonable for the Legion and even less if modern but unused surplus equipment was obtained by donation or at discount. Base overhead for such a small unit would also be small, and if only repair and modification of existing surplus facilities was required rather than major new construction, it could be held to under $50 million a year. Rations and health maintenance and miscellaneous charges might add $40 million, making the total as follows:[11]

Personnel	$ 150 million
Operations and Maintenance	$ 40 million
Procurement (annualized)	$ 100 million
Base Overhead (including quarters)	$ 50 million
Rations, Recreation, Medical, etc.	$ 40 million
Total	$ 380 million

We must also assume that the entire Legion and its air transportable equipment would be airlifted to an overseas location at least once every two years for training and combined exercises or even operational purposes. This could add at least another $20 million. The higher cost of the initial issue of equipment might have to be borrowed from the proposed endowment, but would be partly offset by the lower manpower cost of having the cadre units on detail and other early savings. If the Legion proves successful enough to be expanded to two or three brigades, this cost would double or triple. Infrastructure might have to be added, as discussed in Chapter Four. But even at the highest figure, it could be affordable. However, the long-term financing costs of naval and air support would have to be faced if and when such units became indigenous to the Legion. In the meantime, that support would be furnished by attaching elements of the proposed Quick Reaction

Forces for which only the incremental costs would be reimbursed, as discussed below. The greater and more widely dispersed stockpiles of commonly-used UN military equipment recommended in Chapter Four would also presumably be available to the Legion, thus reducing the need to transport some heavy items.

What Is To Be Done?

We would approach the UN's financial crisis in three stages. First, the UN must get through the immediate 1992 funding shortfall which led the organization's comptroller to warn that it may have to suspend general operations by November 1992 unless relief is forthcoming. If adjustments in UN accounting and accelerated dues payments cannot close the gap, then interim borrowing authority for the organization should be authorized, to include bond issues either in financial markets or for subscription by governments. Concurrently, efforts must be made to cut back unnecessary expenditures and freeze all increases.

Second, transitional schemes must be developed for the medium term which would involve: acceleration of arrears payments by the United States and others; emergency assessments if needed; a significantly greater contribution to peacekeeping by the least developed countries; phasing out of some existing UN peacekeeping and observer missions; and the charging of interest on late payments. Stronger sanctions should be imposed against major debtors, to include denial of participation in the Assembly and Security Council for serious defaults not justified by emergency conditions. As the United States finally pays off its arrears, as the Bush Administration has pledged and is doing, some $700 million should become available through the U.S. Peacekeeping Contingency fund. Part of this needs to be transferred into a United Nations Working Capital Fund of at least $300 million.

For such countries as the former Soviet Union, which simply cannot pay current assessments in hard currency, it may be necessary to develop a system of payment in kind. For example, such countries could transfer substantial amounts of surplus military equipment to the UN for the Legion or for stockpiling; or they could furnish Peacekeeping forces at no cost, except that balance of payments or hard currency costs might have to be reimbursed.

Other imaginative solutions would doubtless be suggested if the problems were approached with an open mind. The world financial community has frequently coped with seemingly insurmountable crises, such as that of Latin American debt. For example, Russian rubles or other "soft currency" trust funds might be established for use by international agencies, such as the various development banks, in the countries concerned. This would be a multilateral version of the "counterpart" local currency funds that used to be a feature of U.S. aid programs. To the extent such funds could be used as part of economic aid packages in conjunction with external assistance, the UN peacekeeping fund could be credited with hard currency assets (at a discounted rate) by the organization using the local currency. In all such schemes, however, it would be important to use them as temporary, emergency measures and to have an appropriate discount on the assessed value of in kind contributions as means of discouraging them. For in the long term, the UN must have its assessments paid in convertible currencies by all its members.

Assuming that paths can be found through the immediate and interim financial crises, what about the long term? We leave to others the complexities of the UN's regular budget and limit our proposals to the financing of UN military forces, including peacekeeping.

First, a large UN Peace Endowment Fund should be established, at least three times the $1 billion now proposed. A high-level intergovernmental conference of experts should be charged with developing ways and means. Like the World Bank and International Monetary Fund, countries could "pay in" capital, under appropriate safeguards of course, or they could guarantee with their full faith and credit UN borrowing in financial markets -- or from the Bank and Fund themselves. Other suggestions noted by the Secretary-General in his Agenda for Peace report are that a tax be placed upon international arms transfers, tied to the new UN register for such transfers (we believe they would be very difficult to track and assess in value and the tax even more difficult to collect);* that a levy be imposed on burgeoning international air travel (which is dependent on peaceful conditions); and that countries authorize the Peace Endowment Fund to receive tax deductible contributions from individuals, corporations, and foundations. All seem worth

---

* During the energy crisis of the seventies, one of the authors proposed a UN development tax on petroleum moving in international trade, half paid by exporters and half by importers. This still may have merit, although it would also face assessment and collection problems.

considering.

Second, the way in which peacekeeping operations are conceived and funded should be completely reorganized. Only a few countries now support these actions from their defense budgets -- which is the logical place for them. This is not just because accounts calling for "foreign aid" or international organizations categories encounter legislative hostility -- although they do. Rather it is because the missions of international peacekeeping or enforcement ought to compete with the missions of national military establishments. Legislation has been introduced to make this change in the United States but we believe it has little chance of passage as an outright transfer from State to Defense at a time of drastic military downsizing. Rather, we believe that the costs should be transferred over a phase-in period of several years, or that Defense should be given an extra appropriation at the beginning so that the competition can be introduced gradually.[12] It should be noted that legislative appropriations for NATO derive from both defense and foreign affairs accounts. The UN pattern should be similar.

Third, peacekeeping assessments should not be apportioned as they have been in a ratio to regular budget assessments, which are tied in turn to relative GNP; rather they should be a percentage of a country's own military spending! This formula would adjust automatically both for relative wealth and ability to pay and for the degree to which a country perceives its security to be threatened. Even one quarter of one percent of such spending, .25% (or .0025) would currently generate at least $2 billion per year on a base of about $800 billion. Half of one percent would yield the UN $4 billion, well above current levels of peacekeeping costs.[13] Such spending may decline in the future; but the high present amounts would help fund the greater start-up costs for the revised peace and security system.

Fourth, the basis on which the UN reimburses countries for their military contributions should be reconsidered. At present, the UN pays a very modest $988 per month (plus $291 for certain specialists) per man.[14] While this involves a valuable windfall for a few of the poorer contributors (who may pay their own troops less than half as much) it is only a fraction of the actual costs of forces from the developed world who must absorb the difference. If the Peace and Security system recommended in this book (see Figure 1, Appendix B) is established, then different financial arrangements will be needed for different types of forces.

For *Peacekeeping*, we recommend that up to half of the annual assessment (derived as above) might be payable in kind, i.e. through troops actually serving in UN missions, which would not be reimbursed if credited to the assessment. Other peacekeeping costs would be handled as they are now.

For the *UN Legion*, the costs are estimated above; but they should not exceed $400 million in the one-brigade phase, and even less during the start-up. The entire costs would be borne from the UN's peacekeeping account, which we suggest be renamed the "UN Peace and Security Budget." Interest on the enlarged Peace Endowment fund could be sufficient to cover up to one half of this amount.

For the *Quick Reaction Forces (QRF)*, we have suggested that maintaining a division or brigade or naval or air equivalent[15] be considered an obligation of membership in the Security Council/Peace Management Committee structure. These countries have the military power and the primary responsibility for the UN's security missions. Providing those forces would be their dues to that club. Presumably, these are military units that the countries would be maintaining at their own expense in any event. The costs of additional training and joint exercises, and providing greater communications compatibility and inter-operability should also be a national responsibility.

However, when troops are actually called to UN duty and placed under UN command the picture changes. The United States, in effect, "charged" its allies for 90% of its extra costs in Desert Shield/Storm. We believe that the UN should revert to reimbursing only the <u>incremental</u> costs of actual deployment, that is, the extra transportation, operations and maintenance, and POL (fuel) costs, plus combat losses. In use until the mid-seventies, this arrangement became controversial because of the wide divergences in calculating the incremental costs. We think it entirely feasible for a panel of UN experts, analogous to the existing Advisory Committee on Administrative and Budgetary Questions, to develop the common guidelines, definitions and accounting principles needed to standardize the calculation on an equitable basis.

For *Earmarked Forces*, too, the organizing principle should be national responsibility for "peacetime" maintenance of the forces, but reimbursement for incremental costs when actually deployed under international auspices.

For very large operations, such as Korea or Desert Storm, special arrangements might have to be developed in light of the circumstances; and this would apply also to particular localized situations not posing a general threat to the peace, such as Cyprus -- which has been funded by voluntary contributions. Consideration should also be given, in lieu of full current cash reimbursement by the UN, to giving a credit against future Peace and Security Assessments for a portion of the value of the incremental contribution. If credited over a couple years, this device would shift the cash-flow burden from the UN to its members.

Some Perspective

Although the sums we have mentioned, a $3 billion endowment and annual Peace and Security budgets of $2-4 billion loom incredibly large in the historic context of UN financing, they are very small against any single national account of the larger industrial countries, especially the defense budget. The U.S. has been spending this order of magnitude on the research alone for the Strategic Defense Initiative (SDI or GPALS).

The benefits from an effective UN peace and security system are also large. If it works to prevent conflict, speed peaceful settlement, and make, keep and enforce peace where necessary, the savings in human lives (even measured in the cold legal fashion of life expectancy times earnings potential, let alone as something beyond price) and in property would dwarf such costs in just two or three potential conflicts. The UN could run annual peace and security budgets of $3 billion for twenty years without exceeding the costs of Desert Shield/Storm!

There is also an "opportunity cost" factor to be considered. A country that avoids the catastrophe of major conflict or civil war retains productive assets and market potential which play a role in world trade and growth. If eviscerated by the absence of peace and security, that potential will be lacking -- and the world will doubtless find itself paying additional costs for humanitarian relief and reconstruction.

In this book, we have proposed some radical and unprecedented approaches to enhancing the United Nations peace and security system. If we are indeed to "unite our strength" for that purpose, we must be prepared for new thinking on a larger scale in matters of financing the system. If it works, it will eventually pay for itself, in terms of damage avoided, and in allowing countries to reduce their own competitive and often wasteful military spending. Then they can apply the resources to their many non-military challenges.

CHAPTER SEVEN

SUMMARY OF RECOMMENDATIONS

The world of the United Nations has entered an era that poses sobering problems and challenges, but offers opportunities without precedent in the organization's 47 years. In order to make the most of them, the UN must change in concept and structure, as outlined earlier. This concluding chapter highlights the recommendations that proceed from our study.

We remain convinced that the UN Charter and institutions are basically sound and adaptable to new circumstances, as already demonstrated, for example, in the development of "Chapter VI½" peacekeeping operations. The critical factor is less the organization itself (although all bureaucracies tend to resist change) than the determination of the member countries to make the UN work better in the service of their own interests and of global stability and progress.

We believe that if key countries, including the United States, are willing to assign the UN greater responsibilities for peace and security, then the organization can develop a system worthy of their trust. But it must literally be a coherent system encompassing many different elements, rather than a collection of bureaucratic and political fiefdoms. The Secretary-General's June 1992 report on "An Agenda for Peace" requested by the Security Council's Summit meeting is a good start in this direction. But even more fundamental changes are needed.

The Security Council

Charged by the Charter with deciding "What measures shall be taken . . . to restore international peace and security," the Security Council is obviously the place to begin. It is composed of five permanent members, the

World War II victors: China, France, Russia (succeeding the USSR) the United Kingdom and the U.S., each with veto power, and ten rotational members (presently Austria, Belgium, Cape Verde, Ecuador, Hungary, India, Japan, Morocco, Venezuela and Zimbabwe) elected by the General Assembly for two-year terms.

Despite this geographic distribution, the Council still does not reflect the real world power structure. It fails to include on a continuing basis the two economic superpowers, Germany and Japan, or the largest regional powers such as Brazil, India and Nigeria. Other regional powers readily come to mind which could be paired with these five in the world of global and regional politics.

The problem is that revision of the UN Charter probably cannot be accomplished without opening a Pandora's box of proposed amendments, such as revoking the existing veto of a permanent member (which several holders would doubtless "veto"), or adding so many rotational members that the Council would become unworkable.

We therefore recommend this combination of actions: First, if the General Assembly would agree, five of the ten rotational memberships might be permanently "assigned" to five pairs (or even larger groupings if necessary) of regional powers. Only one would serve at a time, but would switch biannually with its alternate(s). That way the most helpful regional powers would be drawn permanently into the work of the Security Council and be kept abreast of developments whether or not they were actually sitting at a particular time. As shown in Chapter One, only about a dozen countries really qualify under such objective criteria as population, GNP and military potential.

Second, whether or not it proves possible to include this larger grouping on the alternating-seat basis, we recommend the establishment of a Peace Management Committee of the Council as a "subsidiary organ" authorized by Article 29. The smaller elected members would retain their rightful place on the Council, but they would not qualify for the Committee because they would presumably be unable to earmark for the UN the major military forces that such membership would entail. Important issues of peacekeeping or peace-enforcement would be considered initially by the Committee, whose recommendations (drawn from a broader base of potential force contributors) would then be reviewed and formally acted upon by the

Council which, in the process, would retain all its Charter responsibilities.

The Secretary-General and Executive Agent

The Security Council, as a committee, must have an executive agent to carry out peacekeeping and peace-making mandates. Normally, this would be the Secretary-General (SG) himself, working through his principal deputy and chief of staff, for he is the keystone of both the existing and any enhanced UN peace and security system. In exceptional cases, however, the Council might find it necessary to appoint the head of government of a member country or even an alliance, as its executive agent. But any such arrangement would have to ensure that the UN system and the Council be kept fully informed and involved in any military operation, and that the country managing the action would be performing as an agent of the United Nations and not simply as a national government. However, the goal should be to staff (and select) the Secretary-General as the Security Council's executive agent without resorting to a national agent.

Reforming the Secretariat

The Secretary-General of the United Nations is at the center of UN peacekeeping and peace-making. His mandate under Article 99 to bring threats to international peace and security to the attention of the Security Council permits him to initiate preventive diplomacy. Experience suggests that quiet diplomacy is often more effective than higher profile efforts. Several Secretary-Generals have used their own good offices and personal emissaries to defuse crises.

To be effective in this role, however, the Secretary-General needs an assessment capability and a situation center that might be termed a "Peace Room." This center must provide a setting for confidential discussion with Security Council members, offer a secure, real-time display of information, and ensure reliable communications with governments and UN field commanders. It would also become the Council's crisis management and operations center when enforcement actions were in progress, although more detailed military data would be maintained by the Military Staff. While we do not believe that the UN can or should get into the intelligence collection business, it must organize to perform independent evaluations of information submitted by Security Council members.

The new Peace Management Committee we have proposed could assist the SG and Council by providing regional assessments of challenges to international order, using appropriate specialized task forces. It could also serve as the primary advisory body to the SG for peacekeeping operations and for providing political guidance during the establishment of the UN Legion. It is important, we believe, for the Secretary-General to meet frequently with the Council and with the Peace Management Committee in informal and confidential sessions to anticipate problems and explore solutions in advance of formal public debates in the Council. This is the essence of crisis anticipation and preventive diplomacy.

We recommend consideration of a Secretariat reorganized into eight primary departments, generally parallel to the main committees of the General Assembly, encompassing: political, economic, social, planetary (e.g. environmental), administrative, legal, and peacekeeping and security affairs, plus the SG's executive office. Each such "ministerial" area of responsibility could be headed by a Deputy SG, with one Under- and up to two Assistant-Secretary-Generals. This organization would facilitate close coordination with the proposed UN Military Staff, especially by the political and peacekeeping/security affairs departments.

Chief of Staff

A sine qua non of any effective security system is a UN Chief of Staff reporting directly to the SG and his top political deputies. This position, appointed by the SG with the informal concurrence of the Council, should be filled by a senior general officer of international reputation. (He might sit with, but not be accountable to, any reactivated Military Staff Committee, serving as that body's liaison with the SG.) The Chief of Staff would be the operational link between military elements in the field and the Council's Executive Agent, normally the SG. He would, therefore, be the overall commander to whom subordinate military commanders would report.

The Military Staff Committee (MSC)

We envisage reactivation of the Military Staff Committee as a potential source of professional military advice to the Council and a forum for exchanges of view at the level of Chiefs of Staff or their senior representatives. However, developments in political-military practice and coordination since the Charter was written mean that military views will be incorporated into national guidance to Permanent Representatives in the Security Council, rather than sent separately through the MSC. The MSC could perform several valuable roles, including focusing the resources of the five permanent Council members to provide early warning of nonproliferation or arms control violations, as suggested in Chapter Three. But we do not envision it as being in the line of command from the Council to the Secretary-General to his Chief of Staff and thus to operational commands. They need a planning and operational staff rather than a "committee advising a committee."

The UN Military Staff

The UN Chief of Staff would require an unusual international military staff within the Secretariat. It would deal with assessments, planning, personnel, doctrine and training, operations, logistics, communications/electronics, and have an Inspector-General to evaluate readiness and training. The staff would probably number at least 200 officers, in contrast to the mere half-dozen now on the SG's staff. Normally, they would be acquired by the Chief of Staff through seconding from national military service, possibly utilizing a "nominating committee" of senior retired officers with UN service to request seconding of officers with special qualifications for international assignment.

The UN military staff would help the senior political officials negotiate the "special agreements" with countries for forces and facilities called for by Article 43 and the specific implementation plans. In coordination with supplier states, the military staff would also seek to develop UN procedures and guidelines which would enable military elements from different nations to work together effectively. The actual assignment of forces to UN duty, as contrasted with contingency planning, is a highly political negotiation which must involve the Secretary-General, his top aides for peacekeeping, the Permanent Representatives in the Security Council, and the military staffs of the UN organizations, and of the countries contributing forces. (Those countries would also undoubtedly want to have what NATO calls National Military Representatives in their UN missions to provide liaison to their military establishments.)

The alternative of a smaller UN Headquarters staff and one or more field Headquarters would be undesirably rigid and duplicative, given the uncertain nature of any contingencies to be addressed and the need to maintain centralized political control of the UN military activities. Elements of the Headquarters military staff could assist in the initial staffing of operational headquarters. Indeed, the Chief of Staff might organize his staff along regional as well as functional lines to facilitate the transition from planning to operations.

Force Commanders

It would be undesirable to think in terms of a single pre-designated Force Commander. Several different field or area commanders may be needed -- as with existing peacekeeping operations. The United Nations Standing Force or Legion, proposed below, would need its own Commander, of course. Larger forces made up of elements earmarked by member countries as well as the Legion, would require a task force or overall international field commander and headquarters.

Major operations would require major staffs at the field headquarters. Some might come from the UN Military Staff but others would have to be contributed by countries. To be effective, the latter should be designated in advance and jointly participate in command post exercises.

Operational Elements of a UN Peace and Security System

Peacekeeping Forces

Although not clearly foreseen in the Charter, "peacekeeping" operations have evolved from necessity and are sometimes called "Chapter VI½" forces. With military participation by the superpowers generally ruled out during the Cold War, other elements have been provided on an ad hoc basis by a wide variety of countries.

Peacekeepers are primarily constabulary in nature; beyond limited self-defense, they are not expected to perform combat missions. Peace-enforcers, by contrast, must have both offensive and defensive combat capabilities, although they can also be cross-trained in peacekeeping roles.

The line between consensual peacekeeping and Chapter VII enforcement will increasingly blur in the future. For example, consent once given could be withdrawn, leaving UN forces caught in a crossfire of hostile parties. Disaster relief operations by the UN could be threatened, or the UN might find itself intervening where anarchy prevails to secure ports, or air heads or railroads, and protect depots for relief supplies, as in Somalia.

Once an enhanced UN peace and security system is in place, the present ad hoc peacekeeping operations should be brought under its operational umbrella even though the conceptual distinction must be maintained regarding their consensual nature. In the meantime, the various missions must be continued on whatever basis is feasible. Although once characterized as "improvisation at the brink of disaster," peacekeeping missions have acquired some standard operating procedures and organizations, as seen in the *Nordic Peacekeeping Manual*. UN peacekeeping has generally been successful in maintaining truces and cease-fires and separating hostile forces. Indeed, the "Blue Helmets" were the recipients of the 1988 Nobel Peace Prize. Chapter Four makes a number of suggestions to improve their operational and logistic effectiveness.

A Standing UN Military Force or Legion

For either peacekeeping, or for peace-making including post-conflict arms control or enforcement, or any combination, Chapter Two outlined the many advantages of a United Nations standing military capability under the Secretary-General and available directly to the Security Council.

We recommend that a UN Legion be established as soon as possible on an experimental basis through seconding of volunteers from national military establishments, initially with one air-transportable ground brigade task force. It could later be expanded to three such brigades with limited air and naval support and stations in different geographical areas. That support might initially have to be provided in major part by the rotational elements of the UN's Quick Reaction Force described below, but it should eventually be integrated internationally and become organic to the Legion.

While NATO integrates only at the Corps level, and UN peacekeeping operations have normally been integrated at the battalion level, we believe that an integrated force of individual professionals who have trained together with uniform equipment and doctrines could be as effective and produce less friction among units. The political symbolism of such a truly international United Nations force would be worth the effort to overcome its inherent problems and its costs, which can be held to acceptable levels, initially under $400 million per year.

National Units Potentially Available to the United Nations

Today only states can generate the countervailing power to deter or defeat a determined aggressor, such as Iraq under Saddam Hussein, if that country commands large forces and modern military technologies. Under a wide variety of contingencies the major military powers represented on the Security Council and Peace Management Committee must be prepared to act decisively, on the basis of a prearranged system of "alerts" and extensive contingency planning conducted by the UN and national military staffs. The national forces involved would logically fall into three categories: Quick Reaction Forces, Other Earmarked Forces, and Declared National Forces. Chapter Five provides some examples of how the proposed system utilizing these elements might work in a specific and very difficult case, such as the breakup of Yugoslavia.

QUICK REACTION FORCES (QRF)

Of the total national forces that countries are willing to "earmark" for possible United Nations service under Article 43 of the Charter, acting through the UN Military Staff, certain air or sea-transportable elements should be designated as "Quick Reaction Forces" (QRF). Something analogous to a QRF is foreseen in Article 49. Any permanent Security Council member should be asked to assign a combat division (or the naval or air equivalent) and any country designated an alternating member or invited to join the Peace Management Committee would be expected to hold ready a combat brigade (or equivalent), plus some facilities. Taken together, several such divisions and brigades from a dozen or more countries could contribute an air mobile ground corps, with air and naval support, available on 48 - 72 hours notice; and a second corps with the remaining divisions and brigades could provide a heavier sea-transportable mechanized corps. Obviously, the rotation of elements would have to be coordinated through the UN to keep a balanced mix of forces available at all times.

To ensure that such forces would not be a mere aggregation, key elements would have to exercise together, with staffs trained in joint operations and in coordinating transport and logistic support. These forces, unlike the "Legion," would be national in character, and subject to governmental decision before they passed to UN command. Once deployed on a mission, however, they would be responsible only to the international force commander and the UN's chain of command. They would fly the UN flag as well as possess their own.

Providing such Quick Reaction Forces -- at no cost to the UN's already strained budget when they are in an on-call status -- might be regarded as an obligation stemming from permanent Security Council or near equivalent status. Countries would be expected to assign these forces to the UN in the event of need in accordance with their advance pledges, except in an "overriding" national emergency.

OTHER EARMARKED FORCES

The balance of the forces "earmarked" for UN service would also be available for larger contingencies, whether or not the QRF elements had already been called up. They would, however, have a lower readiness status as negotiated in the various special agreements between the UN and the providing country, pursuant to Article 43. They would also have a lower presumption of automatic availability than the QRF elements. However, the Article 43 obligation to "make available" forces to the Security Council applies to all United Nations members, not just those on the Security Council. This proviso widens the array of potential contributions.

The earmarking process should provide a detailed inventory of military assets potentially available for UN deployment -- including bases and facilities. The earmarked forces actually called to UN duty would have to be subject to UN reimbursement, but under the revised procedure suggested in Chapter Six. They would be tailored to fit military requirements dictated by geography and the nature of the peacemaking contingency involved. Since these factors are impossible to predict, close liaison would be needed between national authorities (and their UN representatives) and the UN's Military Staff, Chief of Staff, and Secretary-General. The proposed system, then, envisions an arrangement not unlike NATO's, albeit for a larger number of countries, to include periodic reviews of a country's forces, readiness, and adaptability to UN service.

DECLARED NATIONAL FORCES

The elements under this heading would consist of national military conventional forces and assets which countries were willing to "declare" but not willing to earmark for UN purposes. Nuclear capable, special forces or paramilitary elements would presumably not even be declared. Such declaration to UN military authorities would provide the widest possible inventory of military capabilities, including the facilities and mutual assistance called for by Articles 43 and 49 for large-scale contingencies, such as the recent Gulf operations. Readily mobilized reserve elements might be included in this category. As a generalization, permanent members of the Security Council might be expected to "earmark" from one-third to one-half of their total "declared" military forces. Although ideally all the Quick Reaction Forces would be regular and volunteer forces rather than conscripts, the other earmarked and national forces, under most national service systems, would have to include both regular and conscripted personnel. Table III in Appendix B illustrates in summary form the character and differences of the types of UN forces described above.

Regional Security Arrangements

Drafters of the UN Charter envisioned an important role for regional arrangements and agencies, but they reserved for the Security Council the authorization of enforcement actions. They even limited the right of individual or collective self defense: "until the Security Council has taken the measures necessary to restore international peace and security..." But the Cold War and the frequent use of the veto to prevent UN action meant that regional organizations were the main source of collective security.

Today, such regional organizations as NATO, the Western European Union (WEU), which acts as the defense arm of the European Community, and the Conference on Security and Cooperation in Europe (CSCE) all have played or can claim a role as a UN regional agency. Elsewhere, the Organization of African Unity (OAU) has not been notably successful in mediating disputes but it can provide a political umbrella for efforts undertaken by a smaller group, as was done in Liberia. The Organization of American States (OAS) has cooperated with the UN in efforts to settle certain Central American conflicts.

While it will take time to convert such entities to building blocks for a world security system, we believe the UN should use those that are available and effective, but without constraining its own Charter responsibilities. Liaison offices from the UN Secretariat/Military Staff could help to gear UN contingency planning to local realities and in coordinating with those regional agencies which do have security missions or potential.

Financing United Nations Forces

The United Nations currently faces a grave financial crisis brought on by the advent of new missions without new resources, arrears in assessments (including nearly $700 million from the U.S.) and lack of accounting flexibility and borrowing authority.

This crisis must be resolved in three different phases: immediate, medium and long-range. Provision must be made for the costs of the new Peace and Security System we propose. The first two stages will require both better management of existing funding and the collection of arrears. The organization should be given the authority to charge interest, deny participation to members in serious default, and to borrow in financial markets or from its financial affiliates, the World Bank and International Monetary Fund.

Some emergency assessments may be necessary as annual peacekeeping costs escalate into the $2 billion dollar range. Less developed countries, often the primary beneficiaries of such missions, ought to be assessed far more than the nominal $5,000 a year most of them now pay. For countries like the former Soviet Union which cannot pay in hard currency, new approaches should be considered for a transitional period. For example, such countries could transfer soft-currency "counterpart funds" to international lending agencies for development purposes, which the international development banks could then reimburse (at a discount) in hard currency to the UN Peace and Security Budget; or the countries could pay their assessments "in kind" by providing military forces to serve the UN without reimbursement or by donating excess equipment and supplies to the Legion or for UN stockpiles.

For the longer term, we recommend several steps: First, as the short- and medium-term problems come under control, build a UN Peace Endowment at three times the $1 billion level now proposed, through special contributions and borrowing. The annual interest could help cover unforeseen contingencies or pay a portion of the Legion's costs.

Second, change the way peacekeeping assessments are made from a scale based on the regular UN assessment, (which itself is based on relative GNP) to a small fraction (¼ to ½ of one percent) of what countries are spending on defense. Currently, .5 percent could produce about $4 billion for the UN. (Standardization of defense accounting principles would be needed, but should be possible.) This procedure would adjust for differences in wealth and in national situations and perceptions of threat; and it would encourage countries to consider UN security missions and budgets in competition with national military missions.

NATO members supply funds for that alliance from both their foreign and defense ministry budgets; and UN assessments should be treated similarly. In particular, the United States should transfer the funding of peacekeeping from the State Department appropriation to that of Defense, as recent bills have proposed. But the shift should be phased in to give the Pentagon time to incorporate the UN's needs in its mission statements.

Finally, the UN should revert to a practice, used until the mid-seventies, of reimbursing countries only for the incremental costs of furnishing forces to the UN, that is the excess over what those forces would have cost had they remained at home. Again this would require standardization of accounting principles. Different UN forces would have to be treated differently: Peacekeeping would continue but with a number of cost-effectiveness improvements, as outlined in Chapter Four, and a provision for countries to deduct their incremental costs (and perhaps some others) from future peacekeeping assessments, thus shifting the cash flow burden from the UN to its members.

Once past the experimental stage the UN Legion would be funded entirely by the UN's new program for expenditures which we would rename the "Peace and Security Budget." At under $400 million per year per Legion brigade, we believe that the new UN budget could accommodate such a sum within a few years, along with the $40 million we have estimated for an enhanced Secretariat, situation room and Military Staff at UN headquarters.

Quick Reaction forces would be maintained and given special training as an obligation on the part of countries participating in the Peace Management Committee of the Security Council. UN reimbursement would cover only incremental costs when units are actually called up by the UN and deployed under its command. The same principle should apply to the forces earmarked for the UN under the Article 43 special agreements. Unusually large deployments such as Desert Storm might require special arrangements, as might smaller purely localized missions. Countries having relatively large peace and security assessments might be asked to take their incremental cost reimbursement as a credit against future "dues," which would reinforce their payment from defense budgets.

A Peace Endowment of $3 billion and annual Peace and Security Budgets (including the Legion) running $2 to $4 billion may seem staggering in the light of UN experience. But they are modest compared to the defense accounts of the major powers -- and even smaller if weighed against the losses of human life, property and economic potential that occur when peace is not maintained. The UN needs new thinking -- and it must think "big" if it is to carry out unprecedented international peace and security missions.

Conclusion

The development of a shared, multilateral system can help to change the mind set of those countries that perceive peace as divisible into what directly concerns them and what concerns others. In this age of medium-range and intercontinental missiles capable of mass destruction, when refugees from war and domestic turmoil threaten to overwhelm territories and governments, peace should be seen as indivisible. A fraternity of thousands of individuals, who have served the UN in military or civilian capacities, and especially in the Legion, could advance the perception that "peace" must become a planetary concept. That is the challenge for the United Nations as it approaches its fiftieth anniversary and a new millennium.

We conclude that a global peace and security system is indispensable to meeting humanity's greatest challenges: To attain security under law, achieve sustainable economic development, and build community with diversity. We believe that the system outlined above is both the minimum now required and the maximum that would be militarily workable and politically feasible in the near future. If the world community can muster the wisdom to support and fund this beginning, then the new century might witness a United Nations system capable of maintaining peace and security largely on its own.

*   *   *   *   *   *   *

APPENDIX

A: Peacekeeping Force Data

B: Tables and Figure

UN Peacekeeping Forces 1956 - Present[*]

(The 15 UN operations that were primarily of an observer nature are not included in this summary which covers only peacekeeping <u>forces</u> of at least 1,000 men.)

UN Emergency Force (UNEF I)
Headquarters: Gaza
Operation dates: November 1956- June 1967
Personnel strength: max. 6,073 (1957); 3,378 (1967)
Contributions: 10 nations
Perm 5: U.S. (airlift)
Fatalities: 90
Estimated cost: $214 million
Financing: Member State assessments for UNEF Special Account.
Source of conflict: Suez crisis; interstate conflict
Initiative: Security Council, G.A. resolution
Mission/tasks: To secure and supervise cessation of hostilities and withdrawal of foreign troops; Serve as buffer between Egypt and Israel.
Prep period/info: Days. Units arrived without ground transport.
Outcome: Success. Ten year peace before Egyptian request for UNEF to withdraw before June 1967 war. The SG's hands were tied (re: Art.99) because of USSR/U.S. conflict. UNEF could not be reinforced and had to withdraw. Mutual consent was lost. Israel never allowed the troops on its soil so all depended on Egypt. No peacemaking procedure to prevent June 1967 war. Fifteen UN troops died during repatriation, which was slow.

UN Operation in the Congo (ONUC)
Headquarters: Leopoldville (now Kinshasa), Congo (now Zaire)
Operation dates: July 1960- June 1964
Personnel strength: 19,828 max.
Contributions: 31 nations
Perm 5: USSR, UK, U.S., (all with airlift)
Fatalities: 234, (198 hostile action/accidents)
Estimated cost: $400 million
Financing: Assessments for a special account.
Source of conflict: National break-up after colonial rule.
Initiative: Congo request for UN aid.
Mission/tasks: Verify Belgian withdrawal; maintain law and order; (mandate later modified to include: maintaining territorial integrity and political independence; preventing civil war; secure removal of all non-UN military, paramilitary and advisory personnel.

---

[*] Appendix A was prepared by Institute Research Associate Lukas Haynes, drawing on his university research at the College of William and Mary. It is compiled from several of the sources listed in the Notes and Bibliography, particularly the UN's <u>The Blue Helmets</u> and subsequent reports of the Secretary-General on Cambodia and Yugoslavia. We regret that we cannot include data on the peacekeeping force approved for Somalia as the book goes to press.

Prep period/info: Hours to days. Units arrived before command structure, logistics or long-distance communications were set up.
Outcome: Partial success; traumatic for United Nations politically. Katanga's secession ended but not Congo's political instability

UN Security Force in West New Guinea (UNSF)
Headquarters: Hollandia (now Jayaphra)
Operation date: October 1962- April 1963
Personnel strength: 1,576
Contributions: Pakistan, Canada, U.S.
Perm 5: U.S. (air support)
Fatalities: 0
Estimated cost: approx. $30-$40 million
Financing: Indonesia and Netherlands paid full costs equally.
Source of conflict: Post-colonial succession and territorial dispute.
Inititative: U.S. mediation, GA resolution.
Mission/tasks: Maintain law and order in territory under UN administration.
Prep period/info: Months.
Outcome: Success after slow start, political transition.

UN Force in Cyprus (UNFICYP)
Headquarters: Nicosia, Cyprus
Operation dates: March 1964- Present
Personnel strength: max. 6,411 (June 1964); 2,142 military, 38 civilian police (June 1991)
Contributions: 11 nations
Perm 5: UK (Infantry plus), U.S. (airlift)
Fatalities: 155 (June 1991)
Estimated cost: $31 million annually ($636 million through 1990).
Financing: Costs met by troop contributing states, the government of Cyprus and by voluntary contributions. ($178 million deficit as of June 1991)
Source of conflict: Inter-ethnic conflict and territorial dispute.
Initiative: Cyprus and UK request for UN aid.
Mission/tasks: Prevent resumption of fighting; maintain law and order; (since 1974:) supervise cease-fire; maintain a buffer zone.
Prep period: Days to weeks.
Outcome: Success for 10 yrs. Reconstituted after renewed turmoil.

Second UN Emergency Force (UNEF II)
Headquarters: Ismailia
Operation date: October 1973- July 1979
Personnel strength: max. 6,973 (1974); 4,031 (1979)
Contributions: 13 nations
Perm 5: U.S. (goods donation), USSR, UK, (airlift)
Fatalities: 52
Estimated cost: $446 million
Financing: Member State assessments for UNEF II Special Account.
Source of conflict: 1973 October War
Initiative: Security Council

Mission/tasks: Supervise Israel-Egypt cease-fire; supervise redeployment of Egyptian and Israeli forces; monitor buffer zones.
Prep period/ info: Days.
Outcome: Successful separation of forces.

UN Disengagement Observer Force (UNDOF)
Headquarters: Damascus, Syria
Operation date: June 1974 - Present
Personnel strength: 1,344 military and 7 observers (June 1991)
Contributions: 6 nations
Perm 5: None
Fatalities: 30 (March 1992)
Estimated cost: $43 million annually ($452 million as of 1990).
Financing: Member State assessments for separate account set-up for UNEF II and since 1979 under UNDOF name. As of 30 November 1991, $23.8 million deficit.
Source of conflict: 1973 October War
Initiative: U.S. mediation over Golan Heights; Security Council resolutions.
Mission/tasks: Supervise Syria-Israel cease-fire; supervise force redeployment; establish buffer zone.
Prep period/info: Weeks to months.
Outcome: Success.

UN Interim Force in Lebanon (UNIFIL)
Headquarters: Naqoura
Operation dates: March 1978- Present
Personnel strength: 5,800 military
Contributions: 19 nations
Perm 5: France (infantry), UK (airlift), U.S. (airlift)
Fatalities: 185
Estimated cost: $157 million annnually (by 8/90 $1.8 billion).
Financing: Member State assessments for separate UNIFIL account.
Source of conflict: 1978 Operation Litani
Initiative: Security Council
Mission/tasks: Monitor withdrawal of Israeli forces from southern Lebanon; restore authority of Lebanese government; maintain ceasefire along the Armistice Demarcation Line;
Prep period/info: Days to weeks. Initial deployments haphazard.
Outcome: Marginal results; military status quo; over-run/bypassed; possibly useful in human terms.

UN Transition Assistance Group (UNTAG)
Headquarters: Namibia and Angola, (Windhoek)
Operation dates: April 1989- March 1990
Personnel strength: 4,493 max.
Contributions: 51 nations
Perm 5: U.S. (airlift), UK (signal crew, election monitors), USSR , France, and China (election monitors).
Fatalities: 19
Estimated cost: $393 million

Financing: Assessments to a special account.
Source of conflict: To create a new sovereign state from a territory.
Initiative: U.S. mediated with Western Contact Group.
Mission/tasks: Ensure Namibian independence through freely conducted UN elections.
Prep period/info: Months- years.
Outcome: Success after bad start.

UN Temporary Authority in Cambodia (UNTAC)
Headquarters: Phnom Penh
Operation dates: March 1992- Present
Personnel strength: max. 19,500
Contributions: 29 nations
Perm 5: UK, France, Russia, China.
Fatalities: None to date.
Estimated cost: $1.9 billion (15 months)
Financing: Member State assessments for separate UNTAC account. Repatriation and resettlement will be funded from voluntary contributions.
Source of conflict: Civil war supported over a long period by outside states.
Initiative: Brokered by permanent five with UNSG assistance.
Mission/tasks: Demobilize multiple armed factions; supervise interim governmental administration; conduct free elections and repatriate refugees.
Prep period/info: Months.
Outcome: Uncertain.

UN Protection Force [in Yugoslavia] (UNPROFOR)
Headquarters: Sarajevo, Bosnia-Herzegovina
Operation dates: March 1992- Present
Personnel strength: max. 13,870
Contributions: 29 nations
Perm 5: Russia, France, Others pending
Estimated cost: $611 million (12 months)
Financing: Member State assessments for separate UNPROFOR account.
Source of Conflict: Civil war, ethnic conflict, break-up of Yugoslavia.
Initiative: Security Council and SG emissaries.
Mission/tasks: Monitor ceasefire and establish demilitarized protected area.
Expanded in May by S/Res/757(1992) to establish a security zone in Sarajevo including airport. Further resolutions being considered.
Prep period/info: Weeks to months.
Outcome: Uncertain.

Table I

World Population

(Mid-1992 Estimates of the 30 Most Populous Nations)

Nation/State	Population (in millions)
1) China	1,166
2) India	883
3) United States	256
4) Indonesia	185
5) Brazil	151
6) Russia	149
7) Japan	124
8) Pakistan	122
9) Bangladesh	111
10) Nigeria	90
11) Mexico	88
12) Germany	81
13) Viet Nam	69
14) Philippines	64
15) Iran	60
16) Turkey	59
17) Italy	58
18) United Kingdom	58
19) France	57
20) Thailand	56
21) Egypt	56
22) Ethiopia	54
23) Ukraine	52
24) South Korea	44
25) Myanmar (Burma)	43
26) South Africa	42
27) Spain	39
28) Poland	38
29) Zaire	38
30) Colombia	34

(Source: Population Reference Bureau, Inc., 1992 World Population Data Sheet)

APPENDIX

Table II

World Economic Product

(Top 30 World GNP Figures Ranked For The Year 1989)

Nation/State	Gross National Product (in billions of U.S. dollars)[1]
1) United States*	5,233
2) Japan*	1,914
3) Russia*	1,622**
4) Germany*	1,208
5) France	1,000
6) Italy	865
7) United Kingdom	843
8) Canada	500
9) Ukraine	426**
10) China*	393
11) Brazil*	375
12) Spain	358
13) India*	333
14) Australia	240
15) Netherlands	237
16) Mexico	204
17) South Korea	200
18) Switzerland	197
19) Sweden	179
20) Poland	172
21) Belgium	162
22) Taiwan	150
23) Austria	132
24) Czechoslovakia	123
25) Finland	114
26) Byelarus	112**
27) Denmark	105
28) Iran	98
29) Norway	92
30) Saudi Arabia	90

* These countries are also among the top twelve in population from Table I.

** The GNP's for Russia, Ukraine, and Byelarus were estimated by Lukas Haynes, a research associate at the International Economic Studies Institute. According to a 1992 CIA study on the former Soviet republics, Russia, Ukraine, and Byelarus accounted for 61%, 16%, and 4.2% of the Soviet economy respectively. (Whether these are accurate measures of their individual contributions to GNP per se is speculative but they are based on the 1989 figure.) The national accounting difficulties in the CIS economies would render these figures unreliable but they provide relative positions in world output.

Table III

Types and Characteristics of UN Forces

FORCE	CODE	STRENGTH	COMPOSITION	SOURCES	AVAILABILITY
PEACE-KEEPING	3	Companies and Battalions as needed.	Usually lightly armed infantry, MP, constabulary, etc.	Ad hoc agreement with provider nations.	As agreed with provider.
UN LEGION	2	Up to 1 brigade, later 3 brigades.	Mechanized air transportable infantry, artillery, air/sea support.	Individual volunteers from all UN states.	Deployable on Security Council decision. Hours or days.
QUICK REACTION FORCES	1	Up to 2 corps, naval & air support/lift.	Negotiated with each country; regular and volunteer.	Security Council permanent members and selected others.	Presumption of automatic assignment to UN 48-72 hours.
EARMARKED FORCES	2	Up to about half of total declared forces.	Per Art 43 agreements. All services. Includes conscripts.	All UN members with capabilities & facilities.	Per Security Council request and national decision. Days/weeks/mos.
DECLARED NATIONAL FORCES	3	Most of national military assets.	All national assets reported to the UN but not earmarked for UN duty.	All UN members with capabilities & facilities.	Per Security Council request and national decision. Various.

Code for Financing: (1) Financed mainly by countries contributing forces or closely involved in the problem. (2) Financed mainly from UN's general or special budgets, or reimbursed by UN when called. (3) Both code 1 and 2 financing, depending on circumstances.

Figure I

Illustrative UN Peace and Security System

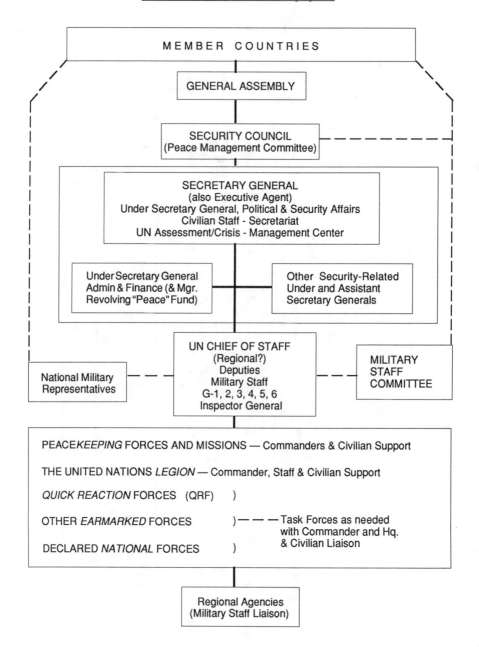

Table IV

Acronyms

(Listed chronologically for missions referred to in Chapter Four)

Peacekeeping Forces

UNEF I	First United Nations Emergency Force
ONUC	United Nations Operation in the Congo
UNSF	United Nations Security Force in West New Guinea²
UNFICYP*	United Nations Peacekeeping Force in Cyprus
UNEF II	Second United Nations Emergency Force
UNDOF*	United Nations Disengagement Observer Force
UNIFIL*	United Nations Interim Force in Lebanon
UNTAG	United Nations Transition Assistance Group in Namibia
UNTAC*	United Nations Transitional Authority in Cambodia³
UNPROFOR*	United Nations Protection Force (in Yugoslavia)

Peacekeeping Observer Missions

UNTSO*	United Nations Truce Supervision Organization
UNMOGIP*	United Nations Military Observer Group in India and Pakistan
UNOGIL	United Nations Observation Group in Lebanon
UNYOM	United Nations Yemen Observation Mission
UNIPOM	United Nations India-Pakistan Observation Mission
UNGOMAP	United Nations Good Offices Mission in Afghanistan and Pakistan
UNIIMOG	United Nations Iran-Iraq Military Observer Group
UNAVEM I	First United Nations Angola Verification Mission
ONUVEN	United Nations Observer Mission to Verify the Electoral Process in Nicaragua
ONUCA	United Nations Observer Group in Central America
ONUVEH	United Nations Observer Group for the Verification of the Elections in Haiti
UNIKOM*	United Nations Iraq-Kuwait Observation Mission
UNAVEM II*	Second United Nations Angola Verification Mission
ONUSAL*	United Nations Observer Mission in El Salvador
MINURSO*	United Nations Mission for the Referendum in Western Sahara

---

* Missions still operational as of August 1992

NOTES

Preface

1. A transcript of the proceedings at this April 22-23 Forum is available from the NGO Committee on Disarmament, Inc., 777 United Nations Plaza, New York, N.Y. 10017. The panel at which the Institute's advance summary was discussed was chaired by Dr. Enid C.B. Schoettle of the Council of Foreign Relations, and included Professor F. T. Liu of the International Peace Academy, The Honorable Geoffrey A.H. Pearson, former Canadian Ambassador for Disarmament, and Dr. Stanley.

2. Parts of the Institute's work on this topic have been incorporated into a recent report of the National Capital Area Division of the United Nations Association of the U.S.A., of which Dr. Stanley is Vice President for Policy. See "The Common Defense: Peace and Security in a Changing World" (UNA-NCA, Washington, June 1992).

3. This was published as "Strengthening United Nations Peacekeeping and Peacemaking: A Summary," International Economic Studies Institute, Washington, April 1992.

Overview

1. See Joseph Preston Baratta, International Peacekeeping: History and Strengthening, The Center for UN Reform Education, Washington, D.C., November 1989, pp. 76-90 for a thorough discussion of past proposals by such individuals as Mikhail Gorbachev, Vladimir Petrovsky, Cyrus Vance, Grenville Clark, Louis B. Sohn, Trygve Lie, and Kingman Brewster; and such organizations as the United Nations Association of the U.S.A., the Campaign for U.N. Reform, the World Association for World Federation, and the Palme Commission.

2. General Assembly, A/47/277, Security Council S/24111, 17 June 1992.

3. This requirement of UN international servants is prescribed by Article 100 of the Charter.

Chapter One

1. See "What Kind of World and Whose Order," Canadian Institute for International Peace and Security, Peace and Security Roundtable, Ottawa, Spring 1991, p.3.

2. Joseph S. Nye, Jr., "What New World Order?," Foreign Affairs, Spring 1992, p. 83.

3. See for example Jean-Francois Revel's most recent book, Le Regain Democratique, Fayard, Paris, 1992.

4. "...respect for human rights...is also an integral part of international peace and security," Hungary's representative said; "Therefore it is indispensable for the Security Council to take resolute action to defend and protect these rights." Provisional Record of the 3046th meeting of the Security Council, January 31, 1992, p. 115 (UN, New York, 1992). See also the statements of Boris Yeltsin and John Major in that record.

5. Jonathan Dean and Kurt Gottfried, "A Program for World Nuclear Security," Union of Concerned Scientists, Cambridge, 1992. Iraq is a special case in which the UN already had jurisdiction by virtue of the Security Council resolutions following the cease-fire.

6. For discussion, see: United Nations Association, National Capital Area, "The Common Defense: Peace and Security in a Changing World," (Washington, 1992) Chapters 2 and 4.

7. Richard N. Gardner, "Collective Security and the New World Order: What Role for the United Nations?" unpublished paper, Columbia University, New York, 1991.

8. The United Nations Association of the U.S.A. annually publishes a Global Agenda on the issues before each General Assembly (University Press of America, Lanham, Md.) which is a good source on these other questions.

9. It is of interest that Democratic presidential candidate Governor Bill Clinton in a major foreign policy speech mentioned "a U.N. Rapid Deployment Force that could be used for purposes beyond traditional peacekeeping, such as standing guard at the borders of countries threatened by aggression; preventing attacks on civilians; providing humanitarian relief; and combatting terrorism and drug trafficking." See: "A New Covenant for American Security," Georgetown University, Washington, December 12, 1991, p.6.

10. For a review of these and other viewpoints see: Jeffrey Laurenti, "The Common Defense: Peace and Security in a Changing World," United Nations Association of the U.S.A., briefing book for the Global Policy Project (New York, 1992), Chapter 3. The advance summary of the present book, issued in April 1992, used a broadened definition of "peacemaking" (for which there is some basis in the Charter) to include enforcement as well as diplomatic measures. This usage was widely criticized when the summary was presented at the UN and elsewhere, and we have therefore retained the specialized terminology of the UN practice in this book.

11. An articulate presentation of this viewpoint can be found in F.T. Liu, United Nations Peacekeeping and the Non-Use of Force, International Peace Academy, Occasional Paper, New York, 1992. Its author spent 37 years in the UN Secretariat dealing with peacekeeping and retired as Assistant Secretary General for Special Political Affairs.

12. Table II is derived from different sources to get a common year and Gross National Product -- a better measure than GDP because foreign trade is included. These sources vary somewhat but the magnitudes are comparable. Conversion to dollars is by purchasing power parities in most cases, but by exchange rates where purchasing power conversion is unavailable.

13. Using data from the current Strategic Balance, International Institute for Strategic Studies, London, 1992, we consider as "substantial" military forces exceeding 200,000. Judgements of power projection capability are more subjective but are based on an estimated ability to deploy and sustain at least a division force, with corps-type support, in a contiguous foreign area without the use of reserves. For countries with total forces approximating only 100,000, the estimate is for a brigade-level unit with divisional-type support. Air or sealift for out-of-area deployments are assumed to be provided by other countries.

14. See UN Document S/PV 3046, p. 111.

15. Ibid. p. 144.

16. A review of the early period of North-South antagonism can be found in Timothy W. Stanley: "International Codes of Conduct for MNC's: A Skeptical View of the Process," American University Law Review, Vol. 30, No. 4 (1981) and in S.M. Rosenblatt and T.W. Stanley, Eds., Technology and Economic Development: A Realistic Perspective (Westview Press: Boulder, CO, 1979) for the International Economic Studies Institute.

17. Thomas R. Pickering, "Power and Purpose, Making Multilateralism Work," Foreign Service Journal, July 1992.

18. For an excellent journalistic description of the process see, John Newhouse: "The Diplomatic Round: In a New Era and Groping," The New Yorker, December 16, 1991, p.90.

19. All references to the January 31, 1992 Security Council Summit are to the Provisional Verbatim Record, UN S/PV 3046, 1992.

20. The Washington Post, February 20, 1992, p. A1.

21. The New York Times, February 22, 1992, p. 1.

22. The changes from the February 18 to the April 16 drafts are analyzed in detail in The Washington Post and The New York Times editions of Sunday, May 24, 1992. See also The Washington Times, June 8, 1992.

23. See "France, Germany Unveil Corps as Step Toward European Defense," The Washington Post, May 23, 1992, p. A15.

24. The New York Times, June 5, 1992, p.1.

25. In his New York Times column of May 22, 1992, A.M. Rosenthal writes: "The disaster of Yugoslavia, once a nation, now a scream of agony, should have been crisis enough to persuade the leaders of the new Europe to put up or shut up. They do neither...they look around for United States help without enough guts to admit it."

Chapter Two

1. See "An Agenda for Peace," United Nations, New York, June 1992 (Doc. A/47/277, S/24111) especially p. 13.

2. One long-time backer of SDI has proposed that centrally controlling national components of a GPALS become a NATO mission. See Brig. Gen. Robert C. Richardson, USAF, (Ret.) unpublished paper, Washington, D.C., 1991. If this is technically feasible, there seems no reason why NATO (or the Cooperation Council involving the former USSR states) could not be the executive agent for a still larger entity, the UN Security Council itself.

3. Chapter Four contains a suggestion for such "recruiting."

4. "An Agenda for Peace," cited above.

5. This principle of equality was in fact the basis for all the preliminary work done by the Military Staff Committee in 1946-47 at Soviet and Chinese insistence.

Chapter Three

1. There is an extensive literature going back many years on this subject, including professional journals, notably International Organization, Cambridge, MA: MIT Press, Quarterly. Among the more useful books published in America on the United Nations are Leland M.Goodrich and Anne Simons, The United Nations and the Maintenance of International Peace and Security, Brookings Institution, Washington, 1955; Stephen S. Goodspeed, The Nature and Function of International Organization, Oxford University Press, Oxford, 1959; and Arthur N. Holcombe, Chairman, Strengthening the United Nations: Report of the Commission to Study the Organization of Peace, Harper & Brothers, New York, 1957.

2. UN Doc S/23500 of January 31, 1992.

3. The Permanent Representatives at the North Atlantic Council recognized the need for a Situation Center after their experience of dealing with the Cuban missile crisis. The only room available as a makeshift crisis center for a restricted meeting with photos, maps and charts was the NATO Secretary General's conference room. After a ministerial review inspired numerous high tech reforms, the first Situation Room was built in the Headquarters at Paris. The present, more elaborate facility is a central part of the civil headquarters near Brussels.

4. Leland M. Goodrich and Edvard Hambro, Charter of the United Nations: Commentary and Documents, World Peace Foundation, Boston, 1946, pp 182-184.

Chapter Four

1. For more complete analysis of past UN peacekeeping see The Blue Helmets: A Review of United Nations Peacekeeping, 2nd Edition, United Nations, New York, 1990.

2. Numerous articles in The New York Times and The Washington Post during the summer of 1992 described the hazards that UNPROFOR and detachments to Bosnia-Herzegovina faced in war-torn Yugoslavia. UN commander, Major-General Lewis MacKenzie was particularly outspoken on this subject.

3. We do not cover non-UN peacekeeping coalitions in this chapter. Numerous multinational forces have been put together over the years. These include: the Arab Deterrent Force in Lebanon from 1976-1983; the Multilateral Force and Observers in the Sinai in 1982; the Multinational Force in Beirut from 1982-84; the Symbolic Arab Security Force in Lebanon in 1976; the Commonwealth Monitoring Force in Rhodesia in 1979; the Indian Peacekeeping Force in Sri Lanka from 1987-1990; and the Economic Community of West African States Monitoring Group in Liberia from 1990-92.

4. William J. Durch and Barry M. Blechman, Keeping the Peace: The United Nations In The Emerging World Order, The Henry L. Stimson Center, Washington, D.C., March 1992, pp. 41-

42. This source was a major reference for Section I of Chapter Four.

5. Reference to preventive deployment can be found in the remarks of Professor Louis B. Sohn before the Smithsonian Resident Associate Program, Hirshhorn Museum, Washington, D.C., July 16, 1992.

6. See Joseph Preston Baratta, International Peacekeeping: History and Strengthening, The Center for UN Reform Education, Washington, D.C., November 1989, p. 98.

7. On July 15, 1948, the Security Council passed resolution #54, ordering a second truce in Palestine. Failure to comply, the resolution stated "would demonstrate the existence of a breach of the peace within the meaning of Article 39 of the Charter requiring immediate consideration by the Security Council with a view to such further action under Chapter VII of the Charter as may be decided upon by the Council." This resolution allowed the UNTSO operation to remain, which it has, for more than forty years, despite several military conflicts.

8. UN Document S/Res/689/April 9, 1991.

9. See Thomas G. Weiss and Jarat Chopra, United Nations Peacekeeping: An ACUNS Teaching Text, The Academic Council on the United Nations System, Washington, 1992, for an extensive bibliography on peacekeeping. In addition to a long list of pre-Gulf War studies, the new cooperation in the Security Council has produced a number of new forums for review. The General Accounting Office of the U.S. Congress is in the process of reviewing UN peacekeeping practices. The U.S. Commission on Improving the Effectiveness of the UN has just convened in Washington and the UN Special Committee on Peacekeeping continues to issue its own recommendations.

10. A request for re-circulation of this report was made by the Special Committee on Peacekeeping Operations, 109th Meeting, GA/PK/111 June 1, 1992.

11. The authors would like to thank Walter Dorn for sharing the recommendations in his excellent dissertation draft, "Keeping Watch For Peace: Fact-Finding By the UN Secretary-General," Toronto, March 1991.

12. U.S. Assistant Secretary of State John Bolton, testifying before Congress in June 1992 addressed the new demand for peacekeeping operations and resources: "new peacekeeping missions must have clearly defined mandates, specific time frames for operation and be as lean and efficient as possible."

13. The operation in the Congo (ONUC) is the best example of operations doomed by political conflict in the Security Council. But mandates with full support may not always succeed either. Some operations, namely those attempting to monitor arms trafficking, in Lebanon in 1958 (UNOGIL), Yemen in 1963 (UNYOM) and Central America in 1989 (ONUCA), fail because their mandate doesn't provide necessary access, equipment or strength.

14. See Baratta, cited, p. 92.

15. Urquhart, Brian, A Life in Peace and War, New York, Harper & Row, 1987.

16. Fabian, Larry, Soldiers Without Enemies, Brookings Institution, Washington, 1971.

17. The difficult question of how to reinforce peacekeepers is only now receiving the serious consideration it deserves. See F.T. Liu, United Nations Peacekeeping and the Non-Use of Force, International Peace Academy, New York, 1992; as well as Weiss and Chopra, cited, especially p. 42; for excellent discussions on the use of force by UN peacekeepers.

Chapter Four, Part II

1. The authors are much indebted to retired U.S. Foreign Service Officer Edgar Beigel for sharing his extensive knowledge with us and reviewing an initial draft. Other sources include periodic articles in The New York Times, The Washington Post, and Le Monde, especially for January 15, 1985, April 22, 1989, and May 21 and May 22, 1992.

2. The Washington Post, May 23, 1992, p. A15.

3. See "U.S.- French Tensions Called Peril to Alliance," The Washington Post, May 27, 1992, p. A21.

4. The North Atlantic Treaty Organization: Facts and Figures, published by the NATO Information Service (Brussels, Eleventh Edition, 1989) is the authoritative source. See especially Chapter 4. Two scholarly analyses are: Robert E. Osgood, NATO: The Entangling Alliance (University of Chicago Press, Chicago, 1962) and Timothy W. Stanley, NATO in Transition, (Praeger, for the Council on Foreign Relations, New York, 1965).

5. This is because of the Treaty's Article 5 language calling for action "individually or collectively and in concert with the other Parties" to restore security. The UN Charter also confirms in Article 51 "the inherent right of individual or collective self-defense."

6. This was put to the test when France withdrew from the military side of the alliance in 1966 and expelled U.S. and other allied forces from its territory. For a time, the international staff felt that it could not make plans for the remaining 14 members. But under the leadership of the dean of the NATO diplomatic corps, the "Fourteen" did organize themselves to get the job done, including the complex relocation to Belgium and the adoption of the "flexible response" strategy, with delegations taking the chair of various Council committees. In fact, one of the co-authors served for a time as de facto Assistant Secretary General for Defense Planning as well as the U.S. representative. Eventually, the French made it known that they had no objection to NATO acting without them through the Defense Planning Committee of the Council, and the Alliance proceeded successfully on this basis for many years.

7. See Stanley, cited, especially Chapter 7, and NATO Facts and Figures, pages 67-73 for details of these developments.

8. See NATO, cited, Chapters 12 and 18 for an authoritative and detailed account.

9. This principle presented an interesting problem when France withdrew from the military side of the alliance before it could legally have done so from the treaty itself. Also allied forces were forced to vacate facilities in France which had been funded by the U.S. or by the NATO

infrastructure program. Two claims by the U.S. and NATO respectively were presented to the French, who initially took no action at all. Some years later, however, to the surprise of many, the French government quietly settled these claims (for about half the amounts asked) by a series of payments.

10. This brief description draws on NATO Facts and Figures, cited, p. 351-352.

11. The authors are indebted to Rear Admiral Klaus-Dieter Laudien of Germany, recent Commander of the SNFA, for sharing his knowledge and experience on this subject. See also NATO Facts and Figures, p. 352.

12. Years later, one of the co-authors represented the U.S. Arms Control and Disarmament Agency at the opening of the negotiations in Vienna on Mutual and Balanced Force Reductions (MBFR), which later became the Conventional Forces in Europe (CFE) negotiations. At first, social mixing of East and West was decidedly sticky, for it was the first time since Athens and Sparta that two hostile alliance systems had negotiated with each other. At one early dinner, the host suggested some group singing; but few songs were common to Poles, Norwegians, Americans, Russians, Czechs and the British. One of them, it turned out, was Tom Lehrer's satirical piece "The MLF Lullaby" -- which did indeed break the ice!

13. Robert von Pagenhardt "Toward An Atlantic Defense Community: The First Effort, 1960-1966," Doctoral Dissertation, Stanford University, June 1970 (mimeographed, two volumes.)

14. The Principal Secretary of the MLF Working Group is one of this book's authors, Dr. Robert von Pagenhardt. His dissertation, cited, provides texts of the draft charter and certain sub-group reports in the appendices.

15. More detailed information and official sources are contained in von Pagenhardt, cited, and in various contemporary articles, such as John Cotten, (Captain USN), "The Military Side of the MLF" Die Wehrkunde, May 1964.

16. The New York Times, June 20, 1992, interview with Paul Lewis.

Chapter Six

1. A good summary of the UN's financial problem as of March 1992 can be found in the article by Enid C.B. Shoettle, "Getting Serious About the United Nations," Council Briefings, New York, Council on Foreign Relations, May 1992.

2. "An Agenda For Peace," cited p. 19.

3. The United Nations Association of the U.S.A. publishes an excellent annual summary of issues before the General Assembly, entitled: A Global Agenda, (University Press of America, Lanham, Maryland.) The 1991 version, issues before the 46th General Assembly, contains a comprehensive review of UN financing problems from which we have drawn in this study. See pp. 273-283.

4. See Durch and Blechman, cited, pages 49-64 for a more extensive discussion.

5. Ibid., p. 57.

6. See Report of Special Committee on Peacekeeping, UN General Assembly, GA/PK/108, New York, June 1992.

7. See United Nations Association of the U.S.A., Washington Weekly Report, XVIII. No. 24, July 31, 1992.

8. World Association for World Federation, Commission of Experts, "A Proposal for United Nations Security Forces," Amsterdam, 1989, p. 14.

9. U.S. Department of Defense, Annual Report to the President and the Congress, Washington, D.C., USGPO, February 1992, p. 23.

10. See: "Financing of the United Nations Protection Force, Report of the Secretary-General," A 46/236/add. 1, March 6, 1992. (UN, New York.)

11. These rough estimates are based on data furnished by staff of the DOD Comptroller and U.S. Army comptrollers. We have beefed up the 7th Infantry model by adding more vehicles and some (Bradley) APC's, and deducted from the 101st Division some specialized airborne equipment. We have averaged useful life estimates of 8-15 years at 12 years for amortization purposes. We assume that normal wear and tear is included in Operations and Maintenance and that combat losses, if any, would be replaced outside the regular budget.

12. H.R. 2560, 102nd Congress. This bill has, inevitably, engendered jurisdictional arguments between the foreign affairs and armed services committees of Congress itself.

13. Ruth Leger Sivard, World Military and Social Expenditures, (Washington, D.C.; World Priorities), 1991.

14. See "Model agreement between the United Nations and Member States contributing personnel and equipment to United Nations peacekeeping operations," Report of the Secretary-General, A/46/185, May 23, 1991, UN, New York, p. 5.

15. Establishing "equivalence" between military units has always been elusive, whether done via budgets with either purchasing power parity or exchange rate conversions or via so-called comparative firepower indices. It is even more difficult in comparing the apples and oranges of ground with naval or air units. One solution, once a given type of contribution has been determined to be necessary and of suitable quality, might be to assess its cost as a percent of the contributing country's operational military budget. Thus if Country A's airborne brigade represents only 1% of that budget (without counting overheads) while Country B's fighter squadron represents 3% of its budget adjustments would be needed to attain rough equivalence. Considerable work has been done under UN auspices to improve the comparability of national military expenditures in an arms control context. With the advent of glasnost in the East, greater progress should now be possible, and the results could be adapted to UN cost-sharing purposes.

Appendix: Tables

1. Sources for GNP were derived from the CIA World Fact Book of 1990 and The World Almanac (1992). Owing to the difficulty of compiling a comprehensive list from one source, the figures are a mix from both sources.

2. Enforcement arm for UNTEA (United Nations Transitional Executive Authority)

3. Enforcement arm for UNAMIC (United Nations Advanced Mission in Cambodia)

SELECTED BIBLIOGRAPHY

Baratta, Joseph Preston, International Peacekeeping: History and Strengthening, The Center for UN Reform Education, Washington, D.C., November 1989.

Boutros-Ghali, Boutros, "An Agenda For Peace: Preventive Diplomacy, Peacemaking and Peacekeeping," United Nations, New York, June 17, 1992.

Cleveland, Harlan, The Third Try At World Order, Aspen Institute, New York, 1977.

Durch, William J. and Blechman, Barry M., Keeping the Peace: The United Nations In The Emerging World Order, The Henry L. Stimson Center, Washington, 1992.

Falk, Richard A., Ed. The United Nations and a Just World Order, Westview Press, Boulder, 1991.

Gardner, Richard N., "International Law and the Use of Force," Adelphi Papers, 1991 Annual Conference Papers, IISS, London, 1992; "Collective Security and the New World Order: What Role for the United Nations?" Columbia University (mimeographed), New York, 1991.

Goodrich, Leland M. The United Nations and the Maintenance of International Peace and Security, Brookings Institution, Washington, 1955; Charter of the United Nations: Commentary and Documents, World Peace Foundation, Boston, 1946.

International Institute for Strategic Studies, The Military Balance, 1991-1992; Strategic Survey, 1991-1992; Survival, Symposium on Peacekeeping, (1990),

London, 1992.

Laurenti, Jeffrey, "Directions and Dilemmas in Collective Security: Reflections from a Global Roundtable," United Nations Association of the U.S.A. & The Fletcher School of Diplomacy, New York, 1992.

Lee, VADM John M., "The Multilateral Force" in Henry Owen, Ed., Gerard C. Smith, A Career in Progress, University Press of America, Lanham, MD, 1989.

Legault, Albert, "United Nations Peacekeeping and Peacemaking: 1991-1992," The Academic Council on the United Nations System, Washington, D.C., 1992.

Liu, F.T., United Nations Peacekeeping and the Non-Use of Force, Occasional Paper Series, International Peace Academy, Lynne Rienner Publishers, New York, 1992.

NATO, The North Atlantic Treaty Organization: Facts and Figures, NATO Information Service, 11th Edition, Brussels, 1989.

von Pagenhardt, Robert, Toward an Atlantic Defense Community: The First Effort, 1960-1966, 2 Volumes, Doctoral Dissertation, Stanford University, Stanford, CA, 1970.

Stanley, Timothy W., NATO in Transition, Frederick Praeger, New York, 1965.

Swedish Ministry of Defense (in cooperation with Danish, Finnish, and Norwegian Ministries), Nordic UN Stand-by Forces, Nordets Tryckeri, Stockholm, 1986.

United Nations, The Blue Helmets: A Review of UN Peacekeeping, 2nd Edition, New York, 1990.

United Nations: official documents and reports as cited in notes.

United Nations Association, National Capital Area: "The Common Defense: Peace and Security in a Changing World," E. Dick, L. Sohn and T. Stanley, Eds., UNA-NCA, Washington, June 1992.

United Nations Association of the U.S.A., A Global Agenda, University Press of America, Lanham, Maryland, 1991; Global Policy Project Briefing Book, "The Common Defense: Peace and Security in a Changing World," UNA-USA, New York, 1992.

U.S. Department of Defense, Annual Report to the President and the Congress, U.S. Government Printing Office, Washington, D.C., 1992.

U.S. Department of State, United States Participation in the United Nations, Report of the President to the Congress, U.S. Government Printing Office, Washington, D.C., 1990.

Urquhart, Brian, A Life in Peace and War, Harper and Row, New York, 1987; "The UN: From Peace-keeping to Peace-Making," Adelphi Papers, 1991 Annual Conference Papers, IISS, London, 1992.

Weiss, Thomas G. and Chopra, Jarat, United Nations Peacekeeping: An ACUNS Teaching Text, The Academic Council on the United Nations System, Washington, D.C., 1992.

Wiseman, Henry, Ed. Peacekeeping: Appraisals and Proposals, Pergamon Press, London, 1983.

World Association for World Federation, A proposal for United Nations Security Forces, Amsterdam, 1989.

ABOUT THE AUTHORS

Vice Admiral John M. Lee, an Annapolis graduate, retired from the U.S. Navy after 42 years of service. The sixteen at sea included combat commands during World War II and the Korean and Vietnam conflicts. He was awarded the Navy Cross and three Distinguished Service Medals and three Bronze Stars, among other decorations, including six battle stars. His shore assignments included tours in the Office of the Secretary of Defense (as Director of the Policy Planning Staff) the State Department (as Defense Liaison for the NATO multilateral Force) and as Assistant Director of the U.S. Arms Control and Disarmament Agency. At NATO, he was Vice Director of the International Military Staff; and at the UN, he served on the Military Staff Committee. In both of these capacities Admiral Lee worked with international military forces of several types. He has written and spoken in various forums on peace and security.

Professor Robert von Pagenhardt received his BA, MA and PhD from Stanford University. He served in the U.S. Army in World War II becoming the Chief NCO for Civil Affairs in the Philippines. After interning as an aide to UN Secretary General Trygve Lie and Fulbright study in France, Dr. von Pagenhardt joined the Foreign Service, where he had several assignments concerned with the UN as well as overseas postings. At NATO he was Special Assistant to the U.S. Ambassador and International Principal Secretary of the Multilateral Force (MLF) Working Group. He now teaches at both the Naval Postgraduate School in Monterey, California and the Defense Resources Management Institute there. He has written and lectured widely on international security and futures research, as well as on the UN and NATO's MLF experience. He is a member of the Club of Rome and served as trustee (and interim president) of the Monterey Institute of International Studies.

Dr. Timothy W. Stanley received his BA from Yale and LLB and PhD from Harvard and served in the U.S. Army during the World War II and Korean emergencies, commanding an artillery unit in Germany. His civilian government positions include the White House Staff, several posts in the Office of the Secretary of Defense (International Security Affairs) and as Defense Advisor and Minister at the U.S. Mission to NATO. In two positions he also had responsibilities for the MLF. He was Special Representative of the U.S. Arms Control and Disarmament Agency at the Vienna negotiations. He was awarded the DOD Distinguished Civilian Service Medal. Dr. Stanley was President (and later, Chairman) of the International Economic Policy Association, a non-profit business-supported group in Washington for many years and is the founder and President of IESI. He has taught at Harvard, George Washington and Johns Hopkins (Nitze School) and is an author or co-author of ten books and numerous articles on both security and economic issues. He has served on three U.S. Government advisory bodies and consulted with several government agencies and at the UN, as well as with business organizations. He is a Director of the Atlantic Council of the U.S. and a Vice President of the United Nations Association, National Capital Area.